CULTURE SHOCK!
Thailand

**Robert &
Nanthapa Cooper**

Graphic Arts Center Publishing Company
Portland, Oregon

In the same series

Argentina	Egypt	Laos	Sri Lanka
Australia	Finland	Malaysia	Sweden
Austria	France	Mauritius	Switzerland
Belgium	Germany	Mexico	Syria
Bolivia	Greece	Morocco	Taiwan
Borneo	Hong Kong	Myanmar	Thailand
Britain	Hungary	Nepal	Turkey
California	India	Netherlands	UAE
Canada	Indonesia	Norway	Ukraine
Chile	Iran	Pakistan	USA
China	Ireland	Philippines	USA—The South
Cuba	Israel	Scotland	Venezuela
Czech Republic	Italy	Singapore	Vietnam
Denmark	Japan	South Africa	
Ecuador	Korea	Spain	

Barcelona At Your Door	New York At Your Door	A Student's Guide
Chicago At Your Door	Paris At Your Door	A Traveler's Medical Guide
Havana At Your Door	Rome At Your Door	A Wife's Guide
Jakarta At Your Door	San Francisco At Your Door	Living and Working Abroad
Kuala Lumpur, Malaysia At Your Door	A Globe-Trotter's Guide	Working Holidays Abroad
London At Your Door	A Parent's Guide	

Illustrations by TRIGG
Cover photographs by Wendy Chan

© 1982 Times Editions Pte Ltd
© 2000 Times Media Private Limited
Revised 1996, 1999
Reprinted 1996, 1998, 1999, 2000, 2001

This book is published by special
arrangement with Times Media Private Limited
Times Centre, 1 New Industrial Road, Singapore 536196
International Standard Book Number 1-55868-058-6
Library of Congress Catalog Number 90-085620
Graphic Arts Center Publishing Company
P.O. Box 10306 • Portland, Oregon 97296-0306 • (503) 226-2402

Printed in Singapore

for
TIN TIN
and
TESSY

It's here. The most entertaining and informative book on how to cope. Thoroughly enjoyable, this book is a must for anyone just arriving in the country as well as for the long-term resident who may be in for a few surprises.

   —Steve Van Beek
    Bangkok Post

Culture Shock Thailand is written with humour—lots of it, sympathy, expert analysis combined with sound common sense, and a deep love for Thailand which I hope you, the reader, will come to share—as I do. I hope, too, that you'll enjoy reading this delightful book as much as I did! And if you *do* suffer from culture shock when in Thailand, this book will certainly do a great deal to help you overcome it.

   —Denis Segaller
    Author of *Thai Ways* and *More Thai Ways*

Culture Shock! Thailand provides a simple, but not simplistic, introduction to most of the fundamental features of Thai culture— religion, social values, the life cycle—and advice on how to cope with cultural disorientation and how to set up house in Bangkok.

   —Grant Evans
    Far Eastern Economic Review

CONTENTS

PREFACE TO THE FIRST EDITION

Non-Thais are an odd lot. Ask those who have been here what they think of Thailand and you will find that this amazing country is both ugly and beautiful, peaceful and infuriating, noisy and quiet, cheap and expensive, violent and passive, funny and sad. If you have never suffered from culture shock, Thailand is a great place to start.

Any human being, plucked from the world in which he functions and feels secure and plopped down into a culture as different as the Thai, is certain to feel a bit strange. Some people cry, others walk around with a broad grin on their dazed faces. Some love Thailand, some hate it and many both love it and hate it. Few remain indifferent. These feelings are the essence of culture shock.

Culture shock is a state of mind in transition, a state in which an individual's senses adapt to new stimuli and he becomes aware that his behaviour, which for years he had thought of as correct, polite and friendly, can be interpreted or misinterpreted as odd, rude and even hostile. It is a period in which his experience of life does not relate to life around him.

Culture shock, like love, is a temporary madness. The most wonderful and most depressing feeling in the world. An experience to make life more complete.

The most we hope for in writing this simple guide to Thai behaviour is to make a few culture shocks less unsettling, more enjoyable, and therefore more likely to lead to understanding rather than misunderstanding.

The path towards understanding is a million lives long and so narrow in places that each man must pass alone.

Enjoy your trip.

PREFACE TO THE FIFTH EDITION

Since this book was first published in 1982, Thailand has leapt forward economically. Change is evident everywhere: the excellent communication network throughout the country, the rapid construction of shopping centres and offices in Bangkok, the industrialisation of the eastern seaboard, the ubiquitous condominiums, the 'iron buffaloes' that not only plough the fields in the central and northern plains but also pump water to irrigate the fields, making possible double and even triple cropping, *and* pull carts and carry passengers to work.

Growth very quickly became an accepted and expected part of life; it seemed that Gross National Product, land prices and wages would increase year after year forever. Then, in the years leading up to the millennium, the bubble burst. Many Thais found themselves out of their new jobs. New condominiums stood empty or half-built. The car once more became a luxury. Furniture purchased on credit was repossessed. Thais were once again sitting on the floor.

The economy almost fell apart, but not Thai society. In some ways traditional life has been reinforced by the Thai response to hard times. Those in need look for help to relatives and friends, find comfort and meaning in Buddhism and express their hopes for a brighter future by appealing to the spirits to intervene in their destiny.

The benefits of social change, or modernisation, that accompanied economic advance have been retained through the leaner years. Immunisation against basic contagious diseases is high, primary and secondary education is available in all but the most remote of remote areas, tribal minorities have increasingly come into the mainstream of Thai life, families are smaller and better able to care for their young and their old. Tourism has continued to increase record year after record year.

It is no longer rare to find a Thai speaking good English. Neither is it rare to find foreigners who get by in Thai. On the other hand, both remain somewhat exceptional. Life is certainly easier for the visitor and the Bangkok-based expatriate: English language supermarkets, hamburger and pizza joints, telephones that now work more often than not.

In coming to revise this book, we have given a great deal of thought to the double-edged sword of modernisation and change and we have decided after all that the Thai personality, which is really what this book is about, has not changed that much. Our revisions are partly normal updating, partly improvements on points that we didn't quite get right, and largely a response to suggestions from visitors, expats and foreign residents to include more practical advice on West and East situations. Thus, the book has been revised, much in the way that Thais have accepted change in their own culture – by a process of addition rather than subtraction.

Much of the addition is geared towards the increase in foreign business activity. A new chapter is incorporated on doing business with Thais and an expanded section offers more material hints on settling in.

We have also made changes to represent better the dynamics of Thai culture. Culture is a game with no end and no final winners. Playing is the thing. Thais play the culture game, manipulating culture in their interaction with other Thais and with non-Thais. We have attempted to steer the reader into the game of situational thinking – to influence how he or she might react in different situations – rather than present lists of dos and taboos (although a reference list of precisely that is included at the back – the game is full of contradictions!)

We hope these revisions will help even more readers to enjoy the ups of culture shock while cushioning some of the downs.

Robert and Nanthapa Cooper
January 1999

ACKNOWLEDGEMENTS

It is horribly unfair to single out a few individuals from the multitude of Thais and non-Thais who helped us produce this book, but not to do so would be even more unfair.

We thank JoAnn Craig who cleared the path ahead of us and guided us gently onto it. Denis Segaller, a dear friend who, but for a turn in the wheel of fate, would be the author of this book. Kieran Cooke who found the antidote to culture shock (a bottle of Mekhong, two bottles of soda and a *manao* cut in four). Webb and Renée who saw humour in madness and made us believe, or want to believe, that there is some kind of place, somewhere, wherever, for *farang* in Thailand.

We thank the Abbot of Wat Kingkeo, the *phu yai ban* and people of Bang Pli, the Staff at the Social Research Institute and Department of Anthropology, Chulalongkorn University, and colleagues, Thai and non-Thai, in the United Nations family in Bangkok and Chiang Kham.

We thank our friends Sirinthorn, who checked many of the facts for us, and Ayo, Sassi, Lung Jo and Souk Jumpathong, for being themselves. And Khun Orachart who helped more than she will ever know. In Chiang Mai, special homage to Pra Santi, Uncle Gerry and Phi Tiu, Ajarn Nok, Phong and Patcharin, Garnet and Tantawan.

We offer our collective thanks to the many readers who have written to us; many of the revisions contained in this edition are a direct result of their suggestions. We will always be happy to hear from new and old readers, who can be assured that any letter sent to us care of Times Books International will eventually reach us.

THE WORD 'THAI'

Over 50 million people live in Thailand. Almost all of these are 'Thai' in the sense that they are citizens of the country, speak Thai and regard Thailand as their home. However, not all are ethnic Thai; the culture and language of the home of some 12 per cent of the population are different to those of the ethnic Thai. The largest minority group is Chinese, about six million, most of whom live in the towns. More than one million Malays live in the southernmost provinces adjoining Malaysia and an estimated half million hill-tribesmen live in the mountains in the north.

This book is concerned only with the ethnic Thai. Most of the advice is, however, also relevant to the Chinese community which is very well integrated into the mainstream of Thai life. Readers requiring greater insight into Chinese and Malay cultures could do no better than to read the original inspiration for the *Culture Shock* series— JoAnn Craig's *Culture Shock Singapore*. Those interested in the hill tribe minorities are directed to Robert Cooper's *The Hmong* (Times Editions, 1998).

THAILAND

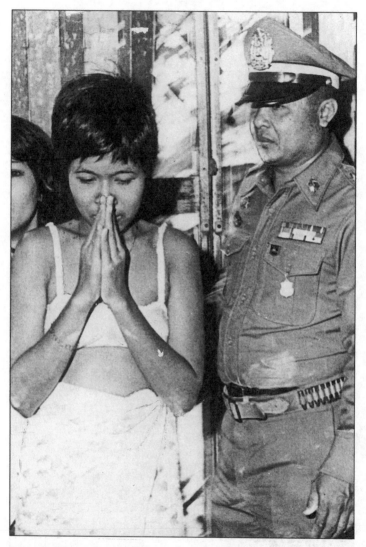

When caught in a compromising situation, a wai is worth a thousand words.

Chapter One

BODY TALK

THE WAI

The *wai* is not just a way of saying hello without using words, it is an action of respect. As such, its use conforms to all that we will have to say about Thai values and attitudes. It is the most significant of the many social actions that reinforce Thai social structure. It does so through public literal demonstration of what we shall call the 'height rule'. This basic rule is simple and clear: in any social encounter the social inferior takes on a physically inferior position and the social superior assumes a posture of physical superiority. Height is right.

How to Wai

The *wai* may be thought of as a respect continuum. The lower the head comes down to meet the thumbs of both hands, pressed palms together and held fingers upwards, the more respect is shown. In daily practice this continuum has four main positions (and many in-betweens).

1. Hands close to the body, fingertips reaching to about neck level but not above the chin. This position is used between equals or between strangers as yet unaware of their social differences (although these differences usually are indicated in some way and a correct introduction by a third party should provide such information).
2. Hands as in 1, or lower. Head straight or slightly inclined. Used by a superior returning the *wai* to an inferior.
3. Head lowered so that fingertips reach above the tip of the nose. Used by an inferior showing respect to a superior.
4. Forehead lowered to base of the thumbs and lowering of body.

In Daily Life

The *wai* is used for objects as well as people and although the pace and conditions of modern times tend to restrict complete fulfilment of respect procedures, it remains a very meaningful part of Thai daily life.

On any long-distance bus, you will notice the passengers *wai*ing sacred places as they speed by. And don't be surprised if your taxi-driver, having beaten the longest red light in the world at the Erawan intersection and screaming on two wheels around the corner, takes his and your lives in his hands and raises them in a *wai* to the elephant-god on the corner.

Buddha and Monks

Ideally, in making a *wai* to the Buddha, or to a monk (the Buddha's representative), the procedure is (a) drop to your knees, (b) *wai* while sitting in the respect position (men sit on their heels, women sit with their legs to one side), (c) maintaining the *wai*, bend head and body down from the waist while keeping the backside as low as possible, (d) when the head almost touches the floor, and the top of the head is facing the object of respect, place the palms on the floor (strictly speaking, the right palm should touch the ground first), (e) straighten the body back to the sitting *wai* position. Repeat the whole thing three times if *wai*ing a Buddha.

Origins

The position of the *wai* shows that your hands are empty of weapons and, in this aspect, the *wai* probably shares a common history with the western touching or clasping of swordhands—what we have come to term the handshake. However, the *wai* does far more than the handshake. Handshakes are between equals, the *wai* is, more often than not, an expression of inequality.

When *wai*ing a superior, the inferior places himself at the superior's mercy. The inferior always initiates the *wai*. Historically, the weaker man would be the first to show that his hands contain no weapons. The lowered eyes and head further reduce the individual's ability to defend himself. The superior may, or may not, return the *wai*. If he is absolutely superior, as is a monk, he certainly will not do so. So, if you are lucky enough to find yourself in the company of the King or Queen and you go through appropriate respect procedures, don't expect a *wai* in return.

Returning a Wai

The Thai King does not *wai* his subjects (unless they are monks). *When the social distance between any two individuals is very great, the wai is not returned.* Thus if a young child *wai*s a senior elder, the elder may reply with a nod or smile; if a waitress *wai*s on receiving a tip, the giver does not return the *wai*; if a junior employee meets the big boss, he will *wai*, the boss need not.

When to Wai

The question of when to *wai* and how to *wai* is learnt from the earliest days of childhood; it comes naturally for a Thai, but is a problem for

Homage to a fallen comrade in the October Revolution of 1973.

the visitor. Having overcome preconceptions about proper demo-
cratic behaviour, learnt the rules and even got to the point where you
can place yourself in the status structure, you will notice that many
Thais, obvious juniors, will not *wai* you. This is not because of any
feeling of racial or cultural superiority, but because the junior has seen
enough western films and television programmes to know that *farang*
(westerners) don't *wai* each other.

The use of the *wai* to say 'thank you' is widespread among Thais.
However, this is not an easy way through the language barrier for the

visitor. Generosity traditionally moves in one direction, from the superior to the inferior; in return, the inferior demonstrates symbolically that he or she is at your mercy. Thus, although equals may use it, the thank-you-*wai* from a superior to an inferior, even if a significant service has been performed, is most out of place.

As the visitor learns a bit of Thai and gets to know more about Thailand, the *wai* will creep into his social actions at the proper time. The best advice to the newcomer might be: unless you receive a *wai*, stick to the handshake with men and use a polite half-smile with women.

When that wonderful day arrives that you meet the right person at the right time and he or she naturally raises the hands in a *wai*, you will probably find that yours are full of papers or that you have a whisky-soda in one hand and a cigarette in the other. In this case, don't worry, just place your hands as near together as possible and bring the whole bundle up to the appropriate position.

While waiting for the habit to come naturally, here are a few tips to avoid embarrassment to all parties.

1. Do not *wai* servants, labourers, children and other people of an obviously lower social status than yours. If you insist on doing so, guided or misguided by an inappropriate desire to be equal and friendly instead of a more appropriate recognition that people can be unequal and remain friendly, you will create a situation of extreme embarrassment for the inferior which may terminate any chance for future social encounter. You will also make yourself look ridiculous.

2. If you receive a *wai*, reply with an equal or more casual *wai*.

3. The safest people to *wai* are monks and the very old (but not if they are your servants or street vendors!).

4. The appropriate deference position is shown by lowering the head and body, not by raising the hands (holding your hands right above your head while standing straight up is not showing respect).

5. Remember: a *wai* is not 'hello'. Overuse would devalue its meaning.

THE SMILE

One thing the visitor is sure to have heard before setting foot in the country is that Thailand is the Land of Smiles. He will quickly discover that this is true. Thais smile much of the time.

Surrounded by beaming faces, the casual visitor often concludes either that he has arrived in a land of imbeciles or that the Thais are a very happy, contented people. The second conclusion is nearer to the truth but is not all of the truth.

While we would like you to go ahead and enjoy the smiles without thinking too much about it, we realise that a day will probably come when you will ask yourself what these people have to smile about. The majority of Thais are near the bottom of their own social deference ladder and have too much month left over at the end of their pay. So, what do they have to smile about?

Behind the Smile

The Thais do not necessarily smile 'about' something, but their smiles are not meaningless. In the west, people smile primarily to show amusement and in many situations a smile would be out of place or even rude. Smiling or laughing at somebody's ungainly attempts to do something beyond his capabilities might, in the west, produce a feeling of insult and the hostile retort 'what are you smiling about?' In the west, a smile is about something. In Thailand a smile is a natural part of life. It does, however, serve social functions and, at the risk of over-analysing and classifying this most beautiful and natural of actions, we offer the following basic list:

1. Amusement

A smile, and often a laugh, may, for the Thai, as for all human beings, show amusement. However, while the westerner generally would not smile on seeing a person slip on a banana skin (unless he was watching a cartoon), a Thai generally would. This does not mean he is unsympathetic; the Thai is just as likely to help the wretched banana-skin-slipper to his feet as anybody else.

Rarely would a Thai smile or laugh involve ridicule, although it may sometimes seem that way to the visitor. One luckless *farang* of our acquaintance was strolling the lanes around the Pratunam area of Bangkok when a bucket of sudsy water came flying through an open doorway and caught him full-frontal. Clearing the muck from his eyes, our hero found himself surrounded by smiles. Fortunately he had been in Thailand long enough to catch a smile as easily as he caught the water, smiled back, and soon everybody was laughing and cleaning the *farang*. When it was discovered that he could speak some Thai, the water-thrower said 'excuse me'.

2. To excuse

In the above example the smile may have been prompted by amusement of the banana-skin variety, but it also served to excuse the perpetrator of an unintended inconvenience. When the smile was returned it demonstrated the granting of pardon. A smile may be used for these reasons a thousand times a day (usually, the visitor will be relieved to hear, for incidents less serious than the example above).

You are in the slow-moving queue at the self-service cafeteria at lunchtime and, having made your selection, you move around people still in the process of discussing the merits of the various dishes on display and join the queue further on. (Such 'queue jumping' is perfectly acceptable and, given the protracted negotiations that often precede selection of food, is somewhat necessary if the line is to move at all.) You accidentally step in front of someone you thought was still selecting, then realise he is waiting to pay. There is no 'get to the back of the queue, mate' (or 'buddy' if you prefer) and no need for an elaborate excuse. You smile, he smiles, and everything is all right. (You should, however, retake your correct place in the queue!)

The observant visitor will quickly realise that the smile is the correct mechanism for repairing minor breaches of etiquette. It may take longer to realise that the smile can also be used to excuse conduct that, in his own culture, would require elaborate explanations and, possibly, monetary compensation. If the visitor thinks he is in a difficult cultural situation in Thailand, he can spare a thought for the poor Thai student in a London pub, standing at the crowded bar covered in identical pint mugs full of bitter beer. Unintentionally, he picked up the wrong glass and drank from it. Upon this fact being pointed out to him in very clear terms, he smiled …

3. To thank

The smile is often used to thank somebody for a small service. As we point out in the section on small talk (page 37), a verbal 'thank you' is used far less often than it is in the west. In Thailand a smile, perhaps accompanied by a slight nod of the head, means 'thanks a little'; the return smile could be translated 'oh, that's quite all right'.

4. To side-step

The last two functions of the smile that we will go into here have to do with the *jai yen* ('cool heart') philosophy of conflict avoidance, the motive for so much of Thai social action.

Some Thais can smile their way out of almost any situation, carefully avoiding any words or actions that might be regretted later. This kind of behaviour infuriates many *farang* but is respected by Thais. Perhaps the best-known master of the side-step smile in recent years has been General Prem, Thailand's longest serving Prime Minister. His survival and popularity owed at least something to his ability to smile his way through the most difficult situations and to get everybody smiling with him. More than anybody, General Prem who had the whole army to play with, demonstrated the devastatingly disarming and charming power of a simple smile.

The side-step smile needs no verbal accompaniment and could perhaps be best translated as 'no comment'; it functions to leave situations exactly the way they are while extricating the smiler temporarily from the scene.

5. To show embarrassment

The embarrassment smile also functions to avoid conflict, but indicates the smiler's guilt and his willingness to make amends. Backing into the front of somebody's car or accidentally shooting a bullet through the ceiling while you are playing with a revolver in a crowded restaurant are potential conflict situations in any country (they just seem to happen more often in Thailand!). A smile (but not a hearty guffaw) can demonstrate your embarrassment and defuse a potentially explosive situation. Of course, this is not an appropriate time for the 'excuse me' smile, the cringing embarrassment smile should be accompanied by a verbal apology and an attempt to rectify the situation and, if necessary, compensate your victim. An alterna-

Gen Prem just smiles...

PRIME Minister Prem Tinsulanonda declined to comment yesterday on Parliament's decision to approve the bill amending the Pension Act to allow extension of his term as Army C-in-C.

The Prime Minister smiled continuously but remained silent when newsmen asked for his views on the decision.

He smiled again when reporters asked him whether he would accept the offer to extend his term as C-in-C or not, and left without answering.

Left: The side-step smile. Right: In place of the usual giants, Wat Sutat (Bangkok) has twelve stone figures like this one to guard the temple. They are said to represent the first farang to set foot in Thailand. All of the twelve are smiling.

21

tive, common throughout Thailand, is to take conflict avoidance to the extreme and 'flee the scene'.

Smiling Makes You Beautiful

This is by no means a full treatise on the Thai smile, which has almost as much complexity as the *wai* (and indeed may be used by a superior to return an inferior's *wai*). Since smiling, like frowning and yawning, is contagious, the visitor will quickly find himself using it. Certainly, he will miss it upon returning home.

Don't worry about the smile, enjoy it. Do, however, remember that the wide smile from the lovely young girl selling flowers on the corner does not (necessarily) mean she is madly in love with you. But smile back anyway. Smiling makes you beautiful and keeps you young.

HEADS AND FEET

We have already mentioned the height rule in connection with the *wai*. Many other social actions conform to this basic idea that status superiority should be reflected in a physical high-low continuum. This hierarchical philosophy even permeates the way a Thai thinks of his or her individual body. The top of the head, inhabited by the *khwan* ('spirit essence'), is the most important part and the feet are the least important and dirtiest part.

Thus, in the not-too-distant past, when subjects literally crawled before royalty, they were demonstrating their humility by placing their most sacred parts (hair and head) below the level of the royal feet, which although low compared with the royal head, were a lot higher than anything non-royal.

In those days, the wretched subject could not look at the king and, being too low to speak to him directly, had to say words to the effect that 'my head beneath the dust under your feet addresses you'. From these humble origins grew the everyday male pronoun *phom*, meaning 'I' (literally: my hair) and used today as a term of respect when speaking to equals and superiors. (All personal pronouns change in Thai, depending on the status of the person you are talking to or about. At the end of your first 250 hours of instruction in the Thai language you will have mastered some of them!)

The Improper Appendage

Heads being almost sacred and feet being something a Thai would rather not talk about, you must, of course, take care what you do with your extremities. As one Thai civil servant wrote, when asked to submit advice for American visitors to Thailand:

THE FOOT IS NOT CONSIDERED THE PROPER APPENDAGE WITH WHICH TO POINT.

Just about the worst insult you can pay a Thai is to point at his sacred head with your lowly foot. This, you may think, is not easy to do unless you are a taekwondo expert, a Thai boxer, or a ballet dancer. You may like to reason that since you are very unlikely to find yourself accidentally committing this unforgivable social crime, you can safely ignore this warning about heads and feet. Not so. Pointing your feet at people or at sacred objects is easier than you might think.

Try to keep your feet under control. Absolutely taboo is to allow them to wander up onto the top of your desk, even if nobody is sitting in front of them. Equally vulgar is to sit in a temple with your back propped against the wall and your legs stretched out in front of you.

A little more subtle than the above examples is the taboo against sitting with your legs crossed in the presence of monks or respected elders. This applies whether you are sitting on the floor, in which case the feet should be tucked away out of sight under the body in the respect position, or if you have managed to find a chair to sit on, in which case the legs should not be crossed. A well-known Thai woman reformer and journalist was physically removed from Parliament when she refused to uncross her legs.

Touching Heads

In the Thai social and physical environment, which is usually crowded and made for people considerably shorter than most *farang*, it is surprisingly easy to touch heads and misplace your feet. If you do accidentally find your elbows touching a head or two when hanging on for dear life to the ceiling rails of a speeding bus, never mind that your own head is constantly denting the low metal roof or disappearing into an air vent, the correct response is to say 'excuse me'— preferably, if you want to be understood, in Thai. Even when you need to reach over somebody's head and have no intention of touching it, to retrieve a bag from a rack on a train or bus, you can excuse yourself, although a smile should be enough.

Remember that Thais like to excuse themselves *before* inconveniencing people, if this is at all possible (thereby implying that the doubtful action is unavoidable rather than accidental). Even executioners excused themselves to the executionee before 'touching' the head with the sword. This charming old custom has been made redundant by modern technology but it is still possible to find a hairdresser who offers excuses before trimming your locks.

The taboo against touching heads is maintained even between close friends but, like all rules of this kind, it is not allowed to interfere with what people really want to do. It is not upheld between lovers. Old people may be seen placing the right hand on a young child's head as a mark of affection and parents in Thailand are not going to think twice before ruffling the head of their own children. However, in this as in other social rules the visitor should model his behaviour on the generally acceptable. Later, maybe, you will develop a feel for the way to do what you are not really supposed to do.

Stepping Over

Because a lot of traditional social activity takes place at ground level, you may find yourself developing a desire to step over people that you never had in your native land. Resist it.

When, having had a bit to drink in the *sala* (community hall of the temple), your path to the toilet is blocked in all directions by circles of people, each circle almost touching, don't step over two close backs (or any part of anybody). It's taboo. And be careful not to step over the food inside the circles; that's also taboo. You can, of course, make it plain that you want to get through urgently (it is not taboo to say you need to urinate), and a gap will be made for you. But your troubles aren't over yet. Don't simply rush through that gap. The height rule requires that you lower your body when passing in front of a seated adult. Ideally, you should show your respect and humility by not being at a higher level than anybody else—something extremely difficult for the average *farang* to do! In practice, bending the body when passing, to show that at least you are trying not to tower over everybody present, is much appreciated.

Front and Back
An extension of the height rule is the horizontal maintenance of social space between people of different status. Superiors sit at the front, inferiors at the back. So, if you are ushered into the front seat at an event, sit there even if you are long-sighted, otherwise everybody else will have to sit behind you. (It is quite usual on occasions where rows of chairs are set up, for the front one or two rows to be empty except for a monk, an elder and any other important person.)

Horizontal social distance is also evident in the order of walking, superior in front, inferior at the back. This does, of course, tend to kill the art of conversation. In modern Thailand, this practice is therefore reserved for ceremonial occasions. However, you could only make a good impression by not moving ahead of an old person.

The walking order is no longer rigidly adhered to but the social order it symbolises is still very much a part of Thai personality; the junior is under the protection of the senior for as long as he follows behind. This is summed up in the Thai saying, 'Walk behind an elder, the dog doesn't bite you.'

THE HANDS

Now fully conscious of your obnoxious feet, your towering height and your sacred head, you must also be careful about what you get up to with your hands. Ideally, do as little as possible with them. Leave them hanging down inoffensively by your sides. Certainly don't use them for slapping a chap on the back or tousling his hair! In fact, be careful about touching people anywhere, and never touch across the sex line.

The safe exception is a polite touch at the elbow, usually to draw attention but sometimes just for the sake of it, between friends and colleagues.

In the office, touching, like every other aspect of social interaction, is subject to the rules of the superior/inferior structure of Thai society. It is quite acceptable for a superior to put his hand on an inferior of the same sex, most often on a shoulder. In the office this would reinforce correct work relationships: it can emphasise that an employee has done a good piece of work, it can soften any criticism, or it can suggest that the meeting is over and that the inferior should leave.

Such touching is avuncular. It is like the friendly uncle putting his arm around a nephew's shoulders in the west and might at times come close to a master patting his dog on the head. Needless to say, the office inferior does not touch, hug or lick in return.

Pointing

Pointing with a finger is less offensive than pointing with a foot and is acceptable for objects (except sacred objects) but not for people, even very inferior ones. Unless you are picking somebody out at a police line-up or indicating to an indifferent public the chap who has just fled the scene with your wallet, don't point. If you really need to point somebody out to your companion and can't do it verbally, do so as discreetly as possible. A slight upward movement of the chin towards the pointee is permitted.

In Thailand, hand movements have meaning.

Sergeant-majors in the army and schoolteachers in the classroom are exempted from these finger pointing restrictions. But, so sensitive are the Thais to being pointed at, that even the girls in the massage parlours wear numbers, so that there is no need to point out which one you want.

All this sensitivity perhaps stems from the bad old days when a warlord would placate a quarrelsome village by assembling the population and haphazardly pointing to a few luckless peasants who would then be executed. Whatever the reason, and however it is done, a Thai does not like to be deliberately singled out.

Don't Wave Them About

Hands, of course, are not solely instruments for showing respect. Some people use them to work. However, the Thai makes very little distinction between behaviour acceptable at work and behaviour acceptable outside of the work place. Thus, even when preoccupied with a work-task, social relations and polite action take precedence over simple considerations of productivity.

Hands should remain tuned in to social protocol, whether engaged in the most thoughtless of menial tasks (like cutting the master's lawn with a pair of scissors) or in the pursuit of the most mind-taxing activities (like trying to decide whether to have *kwaytiaw nam* or *kwaytiaw pat* for lunch). Don't wave them about in an attempt to make yourself understood (special advice for French and Italian visitors); such action is likely to confuse rather than clarify and could give the impression you are angry about something—even if you are, don't show it!

Getting Attention

Two actions that you need to do all the time are getting somebody's attention and passing things. The first does not require the hands, but the right hand may be used. The Thai way would be simply to call, in a quiet voice; in a restaurant you would use *nong* (little brother or sister), assuming the waitress/waiter is young, which most of them are. However, it wouldn't do to call the restaurant owner in this way, and therefore it may be safer for the visitor to use his hand. But don't clap, snap your fingers or hiss. The correct way is to beckon, palm down, moving the fingers rapidly towards you.

Passing

Having got somebody to come to you, the chances are that you wish to hand something over or take something from the person. These procedures are well defined in the deference system. Ideally, the inferior, handing or receiving, should use his right hand while supporting the right forearm with the left hand and lowering the body from the waist. The superior should gently hand or receive, the supporting left hand being unnecessary. Equals may pass something without any protocol, but always gently, or both may touch the fingers of the left hand to the right arm. In practice, the full procedure is rarely evident in modern Bangkok—although a contracted version is still frequently enough seen, if you are aware of what you are looking for.

Always use the right hand when passing, even if you are lefthanded (as many Thais are). This is because the left hand is used to wipe the backside with water after defecation. Although an increasing number of Thais use toilet paper, the feeling persists that the left hand is not as clean as the right.

When passing to a superior, the left hand supports the right arm and the body is lowered slightly.

29

Throwing

Throwing things, even if it is only a box of matches, is considered quite slobbish; if the object is of the 'semi-sacred' category, e.g. food, it is rude. If throwing involves a sacred object, e.g. a Buddha pendant, then you are asking for trouble.

Pockets

If by now you have decided that the safest thing to do with your hands is to keep them in your pockets, sorry, this is considered very bad manners. However, if you are really stuck for something to do with them then you might consider nose-hair plucking which, though behaviour which is hardly likely to endear you to the cream of Thai society, is not as taboo as it is in the west.

THE VOICE

The normal way of communicating with somebody, you will be relieved to hear, is the same in Thailand as it is in other places, through use of the voice. However, since most visitors are unlikely to speak Thai, and most Thais are unlikely to speak anything else, this information doesn't help very much. If and when you begin to learn the language, you will find it fully conforms to everything you have learnt about Thai society.

At least as important as what is being said is *how* it is said, using words and particles to suit the social situation and one's status position. Also important is to say it quietly.

Most visitors will have the time to acquire only a very basic Thai vocabulary and will never master Thai pronunciation. Even those who come to work in Thailand will spend most of their time using a European language, probably English. Fluent speakers of English are still rare, and the visitor will therefore need to be particularly careful to make sure he is understood. The best way of doing this is not to use

... quietly is best.

familiar methods from back home. Ask the direct question 'Do you understand?' and the reply will almost certainly be 'Yes, sir.'

As with most things Thai, the slow, indirect method may produce better results than the rapid, blunt, no-nonsense attitude that is often seen as a virtue in the visitor's homeland.

If you think somebody does not fully understand you (and the chances are he doesn't!) then repeat yourself and try using different sentence patterns, but don't raise your voice. There is a natural tendency to do this, especially in a city as noisy as Bangkok; try to avoid it. The loud voice is impolite and is also dangerous. To the Thai it symbolises a potential anarchic power that could destroy him. He may act respectfully to you if you yell at him, but his mind will be working on ways of getting out of a potentially dangerous situation, not on trying to understand what you are talking about.

THE EYES

The Thais manage to do a lot of daily communication with the eyes and the eyebrows. Looking at the bus boy and raising the eyebrows is enough to call his attention to the fact that you are still awaiting your change. Taxis and *tuk-tuks* will jam on their brakes if you so much as look in their direction. And if your eyes, while trying to avoid looking at bus boys and taxis, happen to coincide with another pair of eyes, of either sex, they will probably get you a smile. As the Thais say, 'the eyes are the window of the heart'.

The *farang* is in rather a lucky position in Thailand, especially if he has blue eyes. Most people will look straight into them. This is, strictly speaking, against the rules, particularly where members of the opposite sex are concerned. However, this is one rule that everybody seems to break every day. Looking into eyes is a large part of the charm of the Thai smile, and the visitor need not fear eye contact. At the same time, most Thais would agree that it is impolite to stare at people (although some long-nosed *farang* are just so odd that Thais find it very difficult to drag their eyes away).

APPEARANCE

Self-presentation is one of the most obvious indicators of a person's status. In the west it has become acceptable that an heir to the throne may appear in blue jeans and a coal-miner during his leisure time may wear the most elegant of latest fashions. Not so in Thailand. A person's ranking, expressed through his actions, mannerisms and speech, is in most cases reflected in his physical appearance. However, this is changing fast. Fashion rules young hearts and if split-knee blue jeans are in, you will see them worn by the more fashion conscious – but not to go into the office.

Uniforms

A surprisingly large percentage of the non-agricultural population is employed directly by the government as civil servants who wear uniforms which carry gradings every bit as obvious as those in the police force and army.

All school and university students also wear uniforms. The sons and daughters of the Thai elite may have a reputation for student activism, but this doesn't stop them being proud of their Chulalongkorn and Thammasat University insignia.

If individual ranking is not adequately registered by the official uniform, a 'uniform' group may introduce conventions of their own to distinguish between degrees of standing. Thus, first year university students, by convention, wear white socks.

Upcountry

In the countryside, things are much more relaxed. Thai commoners might simply tie a length of cloth around the waist if they are men or wear a simple sarong and blouse if they are women. This remains the daily dress for much of the agricultural population (in the north, Chinese-style cotton trousers reaching to the calves and collarless shirts are worn by men) but Western style dress is taking over, even in the remotest areas.

One unexpected effect of 'modernisation' in Thailand has been the spread of the bra into country areas, where it sometimes replaces any other upper garment! The bra is, of course, hardly a traditional item of apparel in Thailand. While urban moralists worry about female liberation, many older Thai women in the countryside have yet to buy their first bra, while many of those who have done so seem keen to let the world know of the fact.

Modesty

We realise that fashion is becoming increasingly international and the respectable ladies of Bangkok like very much to be up to the minute. It is in the nature of fashion that it does sometimes get the better of modesty. Our advice verges on the side of conservatism; if in any doubt, play it safe.

Short-shorts and see-throughs will turn a head or two even during the 'anything-goes' atmosphere of the Songkran water festival.

The visitor should be careful in 'doing as the Romans do'. The lady visitor in particular, if she wants to be thought of as proper and respectable, must keep in mind the image of western promiscuity rightly or wrongly projected through the (western) media and not only wear a bra, but wear something on top of it! She should also avoid see-through dresses or too short skirts. Ignore the fact that much of the female population is wearing tee-shirts bearing the message 'I love it' or 'suck me one,' sexy short-shorts or mini-skirts: unless you want to be the centre of attention, these are not for you.

Over-dressing

There seems to be something of a general, if unintelligible, rule that amount of clothing increases proportionate to status. Thus, it is not unusual to see the Bangkok executive and the university professor boiling under the tropical sun in a jacket and tie.

When it comes to dress, the visitor should think twice before 'going native'.

This, you might think, is taking things too far. Being polite is one thing, over-dressing, particularly in western clothing, is quite another. Plenty of *farang* visiting or working in Thailand manage to survive without the necktie and get by as long as they are neatly and correctly dressed (no shorts or rubber flip-flops!), but be warned that formal affairs always involve the status of the host and therefore over-spending and over-dressing are the order of the day.

Hair

Hair, of course, is sacred when it is on the top of the head. This seems to have little effect on hairstyles which, for Thai men, are often all or nothing, the hair being either very closely cropped or falling onto the shoulders. The Thai of high status is likely to avoid both extremes and settle for something a bit more than a 'short back and sides'. The visitor, to play it safe, may like to copy him. However, convention on hair length, for men and women, is somewhat more relaxed in Thailand than in some other Asian countries. Moustaches are occasionally worn, but few Thai men can grow a beard and the visitor should be warned that many Thai women find beards unattractive and associate them only with old men! The major concern with hair, however much you have of it and wherever it is, is that it should be clean.

— Chapter Two —

THE SOCIAL CIRCLE

SMALL TALK

One of the greatest problems constantly facing the visitor to Thailand is the language barrier; he simply cannot talk to the vast majority of Thais. For most foreigners, to learn Thai to any useful level would take a sustained daily effort for one or two years or more and very few have the time. However, if he takes a course in basic Thai for 3–4 months he can at least begin to engage in Thai small talk. (The best basic course is probably to be found at the AUA—American University Alumni Association Language Centre—on Rajdamri Road.)

37

In this book we have as far as possible avoided giving transcriptions of Thai words because we know they would be pronounced wrongly, and having crushed a cute little thing's fragile little toes with your massive great feet, 'excuse me' in Thai with the wrong pronunciation would do very little to salvage the situation. It is, of course, only good manners and good sense to learn as soon as you can the Thai for the few dozen words that will help you survive. But learn them from a Thai, not from a book.

Thai English

Given the language problem, the visitor will most likely be communicating in English and his circle of Thai acquaintances is therefore likely to be limited to people he meets through the course of his travels or work. Even here he is likely to encounter problems in making himself understood and in understanding. Part of the problem involves the standard of English language learning, which is not high. (Students need to pass a written examination in English before admission to university, but many, even those majoring in English, are unable or just too shy to speak English.)

One of the most frequent causes of misunderstanding is the Thai speech habit of never pronouncing two consonants without a vowel sound in between. Often the second consonant gets lost. This can be confusing; 'I can't go' and 'I can go' mean quite different things, but 90 per cent of Thais will pronounce both as 'I can go.' If you are wondering why your Thai friend constantly tells you 'I am Thai!' the chances are he is really trying to let you know that he is *tired*.

Other words are pronounced with all the consonants, but vowel sounds sneak in between them. Thus 'twenty' becomes 'tawenty', and since *v* and *w* are constantly confused in Thai and the *t* is rather different to the English, 'twenty' often sounds very much like 'seventy'—something to bear in mind when bargaining!

The visitor will find that words that he grew up with, and that he thought of as essentially western or international, are Thai-ised beyond recognition. *Satem* is Thai for stamp; *sanwit* is Thai for sandwich; *bang* is Thai for bank and you take the *lip* to your *aparmen*.

GUESSING MEANINGS

Students of onomatopoeia who like to guess the meaning of words from the sound will have special fun with the inscrutable Thai language.

A devout Muslim from Malaysia, travelling up to Bangkok by train and forbidden by his religion to eat pork, ate nothing but plates of fried rice during the two-day journey. Before beginning each plate, he pointed at the little pieces of meat mixed up with the rice and, shaking his head, pronounced emphatically 'no pork! no pig!' The waiter agreed with him 'no pig' and added 'moo'. At least, the Malaysian thought, he had learnt one word of Thai, *moo* obviously meant 'cow/beef'. But it doesn't, as our Malaysian friend found out when he got to Bangkok. *Moo* means pig. Culture shock is not just for the *farang*.

The Time of Day

Another major cause of misunderstanding is that, although thoughts and words may be translated into English by a Thai speaker, his speech habits may remain very much Thai. Thus, if a Thai arranges to meet you at 'four o'clock', he might mean 4 p.m. or he might mean 10 p.m. Everybody could be greatly inconvenienced because of a simple cultural misunderstanding.

Thais traditionally divide the day up into four sections of six hours each, instead of two sections of twelve hours. Seven a.m. is 'one o'clock in the morning', 11 a.m. is 'five in the morning'. In Thai, each part of the day has a special name, so mistakes are unlikely. In recent years it has become normal to refer to morning hours in the western way of counting time. Evening hours, however, remain inviolably Thai: 8 p.m. is, in spoken language, always '2 o'clock in the evening/ night.' Fortunately, Thais are also familiar with the 24-hour clock (used on the radio and in timetables) and the visitor might be advised to stick to it when making appointments.

Please

The visitor might also be a little surprised to find that, in spite of the fact that they are obviously polite, Thais rarely say 'please' or 'thank you'. There are in fact a multitude of nuances of 'please' in Thai depending on the degree to which you are disturbing whomsoever you are asking a favour from. There are also polite and not so polite ways of saying 'give me' and many other request/order actions in Thai. The polite words already carry the 'please' element. Thus, in English, the Thai may sometimes appear to the visitor to be ordering or even demanding something when, in his own mind, he is making a polite request. While some Thais might be fluent enough in English to say 'Would you mind passing me the water?' some would struggle through a polite, if somewhat eyebrow-raising literal translation 'Help pass water a little' and some would settle for the equally enigmatic 'Pass water.'

Thank You

'Please' and 'thank you' are not used in Thai to the same extent as they are in English because alternatives exist. The most obvious and simplest of these is the smile, quite enough for most situations. 'Thank you' in Thai is reserved for situations where the words literally and sincerely mean that you appreciate something that somebody has done for you. It is *not* usually used for minor favours like passing the sauce at dinner or where people are only doing their job. Thus a Thai would never think of thanking a bus conductor for giving him a ticket. The same Thai would, however, often say 'thank you' when taking leave after visiting somebody at home. Such verbal thanks is a sign of respect and might be accompanied by a *wai* or several *wais* or a bow of the head. It is also likely to be attached to other, less easily interpreted taking-leave phrases like, 'I go first.'

Hello

'Hello, how are you' would be an appropriate greeting for somebody you have not seen for some time, but is unnecessary for people you see every day. The English 'good morning' is expressed quite adequately in Thai with a smile, a nod or, if appropriate, a *wai*. Thai goodbyes can be equally brief.

Upcountry (that is an English word, at least the Thais think it is; it means just about anywhere outside Bangkok), you may find that everybody appears to be extremely interested in where you are going but nobody wants to say hello. 'Where you go?' is a direct translation of the most commonly heard Thai greeting. Think of it as 'How are you?' It does not require an elaboration of your plans for the day!

Speech Habits

Speech habits, of course, have very little to do with sincerity. The foreigner who goes around greeting everybody, thanking waiters, liftboys and bus conductors and excusing himself when he hasn't inconvenienced anybody, may be conforming to speech habits considered polite in his own culture, but he is likely to confuse the Thais, embarrass his social inferiors and could even make himself appear ridiculous and thereby lose respect and status. If you really want to thank somebody of low status, put your money where your mouth is. Tipping a few baht is appreciated (but a one baht tip is to be used only as an intended insult).

Offending

Meeting English-speaking Thais, the visitor is likely to find himself engaged in 'international' small talk. People will ask him if he likes Thailand, the food and the people. Polite answers are usual in any country, but you need fear offending nobody by saying the weather and food are too hot for you, complaining about Bangkok traffic, the number of thieves, pollution and mosquitoes (topics Thais complain about all the time). You are also on fairly safe ground if you complain about the police, unless you are talking to a policeman. However, the kind of 'plain speaking' that may be viewed positively in the west could be interpreted as impolite in Thailand.

The safest way of joking (when you are getting a bit bored with repeating how lovely everything is) is to tell obvious lies (no one would take you seriously if you say Thai girls are fat and ugly!).

If you do get into any deeper conversation and onto the swampy grounds of criticism, make it absolutely clear your remarks are not meant personally. This is often very hard to do; it is difficult (but not impossible for Thais) to have an impersonal conversation on the subject of social inequality with a chap whose maid is walking across the room on her knees to serve you a beer on a silver tray.

By all means talk about the King and Buddhism if you appreciate these most important Thai institutions; if you do not, keep your criticisms to yourself. Remember that even the poorest Thai, although he might have to go to Saudi Arabia to work, considers that he was lucky to be born in Thailand.

Meaningful Conversation

'Meaningful conversation' is really only possible when you have got to know a Thai well. Even then, it is likely to be very different from the version back home.

Although inferiors might seek the confidential advice of superiors in the office, even on personal matters not work-related, it would be unusual for a Thai to burden his friend with the kind of personal problems many Americans consider it healthy (and perhaps even fun) to 'talk through'. For this reason, many of your social encounters with Thais will seem to take place on a very superficial level and to stop before they really 'get going'. This does not mean they need be over-formal. The Thai is a master at appearing relaxed, but relaxation requires conformity to rules of social conduct.

Flattery

One of the most pleasant aspects of Thai small talk is the Thai zest for flattery. Try to keep your ego within limits when everything about you is being praised. Height, hair, eyes and skin colour are all acceptable subjects for praise. Having admitted to being over 40, you will be told you look thirty. Such flattery can cross the sex line (within limits), but try to remember that it is only small talk!

Establishing Status

It is, for the Thai, difficult to get onto anything more interesting until superior/inferior roles have been agreed upon. This agreement is the function of much of the initial small talk. The visitor may be a little taken aback at such frank questions as 'How old are you?' and 'How much do you earn?' Such questions as these are not impolite in the Thai social context. They offer a quick, sure way of establishing a person's status. You may prefer to give a vague answer, 'I earn enough to get by on,' but this is likely to be interpreted as modesty and could be followed by the further question 'Exactly how much?'

You, of course, are free to ask the same kind of questions and, if you really do not want to answer a question, smile and say 'I'm not telling'; you are unlikely to offend anybody.

Names and Titles

Whatever the size of your talk with Thais, you will need to call them something. In Thailand, as elsewhere, friendly and polite conversation usually involves the use of names and titles.

All Thais have two legal names, a personal name which comes first and a family name which comes last. Here the similarities with English end. You will find Thais are introduced to you by the first name only, however important they are.

This first name is normally preceded by *Khun*, the equivalent of Mr, Mrs or Miss, unless the bearer of the name possesses a higher title. Even when speaking English, Thais will use the polite formula, title + first name. Thus, you will find yourself referred to as *Khun* Peter or *Misater* (Mr) Robert or, if you have a Ph.D, as *Dokter* (Doctor) Fred.

Most foreigners (particularly Australians) like this 'first name' habit; for one thing it means there is no need to remember or try to pronounce Thai surnames. Unfortunately, in our opinion, ways of referring to foreigners' names are today becoming quite confused. A growing number of Thais, aware of English speech habits, tend to use a foreigner's surname (with the correct title, of course). This is undoubtedly an attempt to show respect while demonstrating correct cultural use of English. If you like things this way, fine, but you must still refer to Thais by their first names (even to your obvious superiors) in spite of the fact that you are speaking English. If you prefer things the original Thai way, you can point out that to avoid the confusion of being known by two different names, and it *can* be confusing (ask Elton John), you would prefer everybody to use your first.

The visitor should be aware that the use of first names carries with it none of the implication of friendliness or familiarity that it does in the west. He should also bear in mind that the wife of *Khun* Somboon is not Mrs Somboon; married women, as married men, are addressed by the first name.

No visitor will learn all Thai first names. There are simply too many of them. Fortunately, it is quite in order to refer to somebody as *Khun* or *You*. It is also perfectly acceptable to use a person's nickname. This is usually a one-syllable name of earthy Thai origin. Most proper names have three syllables and originate from Sanskrit.

Nicknames

Nicknames are simpler, easier to say, and there are fewer of them. Most Thais have one and use it for all occasions except the very formal. These names mean things like frog, rat, pig, fat, and tiny and are also preceded by *Khun*. The visitor will soon get used to calling somebody *Khun* Moo—Miss Pig.

The important thing to remember is to use the *Khun* for all adults, even when speaking English and even when talking *about* somebody as well as *to* somebody. When you become close friends with a Thai, the *Khun* is dropped and *ja* is usually tagged onto the name – listen and you will pick this up.

Introductions

If you are not introduced to people in the same room or to your friend's friends at the same table, don't worry about it. Introductions are not traditional Thai convention. Thai protocol in no way prevents you asking for somebody's name or giving yours.

A more formal introduction by a third party is normally used only if there is a good reason for the people involved to know each other. Such introductions conform to status rules. Thus, a young person visiting his friend's home for the first time would be told 'These are my parents' and would then know who to *wai*. Relative status positions are always immediately evident because the inferior is addressed first, 'Somsak, this is my mother.'

This ordering is the reverse of polite convention in western cultures, where the most important person would be addressed first. Although you are speaking English, use the Thai ordering; so, if you are introducing your wife or husband to an important Thai, the spouse's name is mentioned first. That way you can flatter both your spouse and the Thai big man at the same time!

VISITING HOMES

Thais rarely invite just one or two people to eat at their homes, unless you happen to be there when they are about to eat, in which case an invitation is essential etiquette. Polite refusal and insistence is normal.

The usual style is lots of people and a relaxed buffet with people coming and going as they please. Under these circumstances, it doesn't matter very much if somebody turns up late or not at all. If you intend to invite a very small number of people to eat a sit-at-the-table dinner at a fixed time, make it very, very clear that you expect them to come. Be aware also that Thais might bring along a friend or friends without necessarily informing the host.

If one guest is prominent, make it evident that he is the guest of honour. Fawn all over him; other Thai guests will understand and not expect you to divide your attention equally between them. Do not be surprised or offended if your big man takes leave as soon as he has finished eating.

The visitor might feel uncomfortable calling on somebody at home without an invitation, particularly if that person is a social superior; the Thai does not. However, Thais do distinguish linguistically and socially between what we might call 'formal' and 'informal' visiting.

The first type of visit involves people of marked status differences or equals who do not know each other very well. Inferiors might call on their boss without prior invitation, bringing fruit or some other small gift. This would be regarded as a mark of respect and the guests would be well received, although the visitors are unlikely to move outside of the 'guest room'. The second type of visit would be more informal and between friends. Both types of visit may be made with or without invitation and specific invitations are rare unless something fairly grand is planned. Far more frequently heard is the noncommittal 'Why not drop in and visit me sometime?' To which the answer is usually 'Yes, I'll try' not 'How about Wednesday week at 7:30 in the evening?'

When making a more specific invitation, it is quite usual among Thais to invite to eat in restaurants. Such invitations will not always include wives. The easiest way to find out who is included in the invitation and how to dress appropriately is to ask another guest, not the host. (If you ask the host how you should dress, he will inevitably say 'as you like' and you could find yourself the only sports shirt in a row of bow-ties!)

Wearing Black

One taboo on dress for the visitor to bear in mind when invited to a party-type gathering is that Thais never go to a party dressed in black. This is because of the colour's association with death. A Thai who is in mourning and wants to go to a party will change his clothes for the occasion. To turn up at somebody's house party looking as if you are attending a funeral will not win you many friends. This being said, when black became fashionable for a time, even this taboo was overruled among the smart set in Bangkok. No taboo is absolute.

In the Home

When you do get into a Thai's house, you will most likely find yourself in the 'room to receive guests'. While you are not obliged to remain in that room, the usual movement is to the space outside the house. Although Americans often like to show visitors all over the house, even into bedrooms, such behaviour is not Thai. However, if you do manage to achieve 'real' friendship with a Thai, you can more or less treat his home and family as your own. He, of course, will reciprocate.

However grand or humble the home of your hosts, shoes come off at the door unless you have been asked to keep them on. To deliberately enter somebody's home with shoes on would be a sign of the grossest superiority and would certainly offend although nothing would be said.

The visitor might, as many have done before him, rationalise the shoe taboo by reference to the bringing of communicable diseases into the home or simply dirtying the floor. (The origin of the practice may well lie in the fear of epidemics.)

Having convinced yourself that Thais are spotless around the home, you might be a little surprised to notice the reaction, or lack of reaction, when a small child defecates in public. Although some wealthy Thais with deep-pile carpets may be tempted to adopt *farang* norms of toilet training, the average Thai would never think of rebuking a young child for such a natural practice and would be rather surprised if the foreigner did so. The Thai reaction is simply to take a cloth and clean off both floor and backside. Thus, be wary of trying to over-rationalise Thai behaviour: your child could happily relieve himself on your host's floor (and even on your host's lap!) without causing any bad feelings, but if you walk into the house with shoes on, however clean they are, you have insulted your host.

Thresholds

The shoes-off rule is as absolute as anything is; even if your host, aware of western norms, says 'Never mind, keep them on,' you take them off. Other customs and taboos are often no longer upheld. There is, however, no harm in knowing that nine spirits live in and around the house, one of them in the door threshold. Thus, if the main door of the house you visit has a threshold, it is polite to step over it, not on it.

A few important doors in Bangkok now have notices in English to request you to 'Please step over the threshold.' This is not simply an invitation to enter. Apart from a desire to save wear and tear on historic buildings, there is a deeper, spiritual reason for such signs.

House Spirits

It used to be customary for visitors invited to stay overnight to ask permission to stay from the host's *phra phum*, the spirit of the land upon which the house is built, who resides in the compound's spirit house, and to thank him when leaving. This custom is still followed in some places, although the visitor would not be expected to conform to it.

If you do stay overnight in a poor person's house in country or town, you will be treated hospitably, but you must be ready to sleep on the floor and to cope with the mosquitoes and simple toilet facilities.

MAKING FRIENDS

Neils Mulder, a *farang* social scientist who spent six years in Thailand, spoke and read Thai and was in daily interaction with Thais, concludes his book *Everyday Life in Thailand* with the words 'I shall leave without having developed a single deep friendship.' Most visitors, if they are equally honest, would say the same at the end of their stay.

Even for Thais, deep friendships are not easy to find in Thailand. Every Thai would like to have a 'friend unto death,' as they call it, but all Thais recognise the truth of the proverb, 'A friend to eat with is easily found, a friend to die with is hard to find.'

Opportunity

Thai society is structured in such a way that almost everybody is superior or inferior to almost everybody else. This restricts development of the kind of deep friendships that can only exist between equals. The norms of Thai society further limit the opportunities for friendship that might be considered 'meaningful' from the *farang* point of view. It is rare for one Thai to bother another with his personal problems, even if, deep down inside, he is crying out for help. The imperative of all social interaction—the maintenance of superficial social harmony and the avoidance of any word or action that could create a conflict situation or embarrassment—makes Thais polite, pleasant, flattering and friendly but does not encourage deep, lasting friendships.

Insincerity

Both sides, Thai and *farang*, tend to see each other as insincere when it comes to friendship. The *farang* who is very, very friendly, invites a Thai to his house, shows him all over it and sits down and talks on a very personal level seems to be baring his very soul to the Thai in what can only be an invitation to real friendship. When the Thai next calls at the same person's house at an 'inconvenient' moment, he is sent away. The *farang* involved in the relationship might complain that the Thai show of friendship was not sincere and only preceded an abuse of property (perhaps borrowed and never returned) or an abuse of generosity or privacy.

Slow Start

The Thai much prefers a polite and fairly cool start to a relationship. Such a start allows any deeper friendship to develop only if the conditions are right. Once such friendship has developed, however, a Thai would not hesitate to ask a friend for a favour, perhaps a big one, and a real friend would grant it. A real friend becomes one of the family.

Blood, or perceived blood relations, are always thicker than water. Real trust and social obligation, as in most Asian societies, is found within the extended family network. Unless you marry in, or become otherwise attached – which is possible – you remain outside this loosely structured but all important family unit.

Thailand remains one of the least westernised of Southeast Asian countries. The patterns of behaviour and cultural values of her people differ greatly from those of the west. Both Thai and visitor might be wise, therefore, to take things slowly, to avoid any value judgements of each other, and to maintain personal relations at the level of 'friendly' rather than attempting to rush headlong into friendship.

GIFTS

Thais like to give and receive presents. These are almost always wrapped up beautifully. Do not be offended when the Thai thanks you for your present (with a *wai* if appropriate) and puts it aside unopened. It is bad manners to open presents in front of the giver. Ripping the carefully prepared gift package apart to see what is inside is rude. Put it aside until you are alone. It is good manners and saves you having to say 'how lovely' when your face registers 'how awful'. It's the thought that counts.

EATING

The visitor will be pleased to hear that eating in Thailand involves little in the way of protocol and, apart from a reluctance to discuss death or other serious subjects which may grace a western intellectual's dinner conversation, no real taboos. No food or beverage is forbidden and the Thai enjoys eating and drinking to the limits of his purse, and frequently beyond.

Buddhist restrictions on taking life do not prevent Thais enjoying meat and even the monks eat meat. Drinking alcohol is a normal part of social activity for men and cigarette smoking remains common among both men and women, although attitudes are changing and smoke-free zones are now to be found in most places.

Snacks

When not eating, the Thai is discussing his next meal, or at least thinking about it. Often, overcome with these thoughts, he has a snack, which is easy to do because there are food vendors everywhere, not the mechanical ones dispensing stale sandwiches that you are used to back home, but living ones, carrying an entire restaurant bouncing from the two ends of a bamboo shoulder pole.

Restaurants

Thais prefer to eat in groups. This satisfies a gregarious nature and permits a variety of different foods to be eaten along with the rice. However, if you have to eat alone it is quite acceptable to ask for a little of two or three different dishes on top of rice.

Thai restaurant owners must be among the world's most tolerant. Except for a few pretentious (and expensive) places, you are quite free to take your own alcohol with you and need have no fear of commanding glasses to pour it into and ice to cool it. It is even possible to take your own *food* into a Thai restaurant, and some hawkers make their living simply going from eating place to eating place selling dried squid, deep-fried birds (crispy all the way through to the beak!) and other delicacies that might not immediately attract the non-Thai. And if one eating shop does not have all that you want, then the chances are the shop next door will have it and somebody will fetch it for you. These norms of Thai restaurant management mean that a variety of good Thai food can be found in most parts of the Kingdom. (Norms are changing; one fancy Patpong restaurant, trying to discourage customers from bringing in their own bottles of cheap Mekhong whisky, has a sign on the wall saying 'Cockage Charge 50 Baht'. The sign has drawn interested inquiries from male tourists.)

One minus point, for the visitor, is that restaurants which are *really* Thai (in terms of food and clientele, not ownership, which is almost entirely Chinese) close very early. Thais eat early, usually taking their evening meal at about six o'clock. The result is that most of the cheaper Thai restaurants, even in Bangkok, close at about 8 p.m. If you go too early, it is crowded, noisy and hot; go too late and there is no food left. The visitor is, of course, no more required to eat at a cheap Thai restaurant than is the Thai, and he will have no problem finding places to eat at any hour.

At first, the average Thai menu, especially if it is transliterated or translated into very special English, may sound a bit strange; cow pat, eggs in horse's urine, mouse's droppings and elephant's penis soup may not appeal immediately to every visitor. But after a few experiments involving raw vegetables, burning chillies and various strange parts of unknown animals, many visitors begin to enjoy eating in Thailand almost as much as the Thais. Thai cuisine is now renowned world-wide and plenty of Bangkok restaurants now cater for non-Thais to the point of spicing down Thai dishes to suit an international palate.

Eating Habits

Eating habits are informal. Most people eat with a fork and spoon, the spoon held in the right hand and carrying the food, and the fork being used to push food onto the spoon.

In the countryside, the fork is often dispensed with. When eating sticky rice with side dishes, fingers of the right hand are all that is necessary, a manageable lump of rice being broken off, squeezed into a flattened ball in the hand and dipped into a side dish. Chopsticks are rare except in Chinese homes. The Thais use them only for eating noodles and *popiah* (spring rolls). It is also rare to find salt on the table; instead Thais use the salty *nam pla* (fish sauce).

Sitting at a table, or sitting on the floor in a circle around the food, you are free to eat your food with fewer protocol restrictions than exist back home. (It is, however, considered odd to eat when standing or walking; unless, of course, you are at a cocktail party.)

As in most cultures, it is not polite to talk with the mouth full or to lick fingers and it is not done to appear to be too greedy although it is normal to show that you appreciate the food by eating enough of it. The fact that it is all there in front of you means you can pick and choose as you wish and you don't have to worry that another course is coming or not coming. When you have finished the rice on your plate, it is probable that somebody will offer you more; if they don't, you can simply serve yourself. Compliments about the quality of the food are in order, and you should have no problem sounding sincere. Thais do not expect westerners to be able to eat hot food (some Thai food is very hot!) and you need feel no embarrassment about refusing something that is too hot for you; in fact, it is sensible to do so.

PAYING

You do not, of course, offer to pay for a meal if somebody has invited you to eat at his house. In Thailand, the same convention applies to eating out: *the inviter pays.*

This rule is clear enough between Thais, and should be readily understood by the visitor; if you like somebody enough to invite them to eat, then you foot the bill. There are, however, many situations where no clear invitation has been made. In this case the rule is: *the superior pays.*

If the eating/drinking circle is composed of near equals (or if you would like to think it is), it is still not Thai custom to 'go Dutch'. The value placed on generosity means that somebody will offer to pay, preferably you. The moment to make this offer is when everybody is ready to leave. Learn fast the Thai for 'bill please', so that, having ensured all have had enough, you can simply ask the waitress and she will bring the bill to you. (The word 'bill' or *bin* will be readily understood in most Bangkok restaurants.) A man who repeatedly fails to pay, or acts in a way that would confuse and even insult his Thai companions, by offering to reimburse the payer for *his share alone*, would be thought of as *mean*; Thais would refer to him as *khi nio*, which can be translated as 'sticky shit,' the implication perhaps being that it is very difficult to get anything out of him! Such a reputation would not only damage your social life but would seriously affect your social status.

Paying for the group is such an established norm that if you board a bus with friends and, as often happens, you get physically separated by the ebb and flow of the crowd, your friends, upon seeing you pay the bus boy, will ignore him when he gets to them. If you find yourself frequently in the position of the superior, at least when the time comes to pay, console yourself with the thought that Thais are treating you with respect by allowing you to treat them with food. If this sounds a bit too much like buying respect and status, then you are already beginning to understand the Thai system.

SEXUAL INTERACTION

Ideal female behaviour (ideal, that is, in the eyes of a Thai man) may be best described by citing at some length translated pieces from *A Maxim for Ladies* (*Ovaht Krasattri*), written in 1844 by Sunthorn Phu, a famous Thai poet who continues to form part of the school curriculum and whose 'advice to women' continues to be wistfully cited by Thai romantics.

Walk slowly. While walking, do not swing your arms too much ... do not sway your breasts, do not run fingers through your hair, and don't talk ...

Do not stare at anything, particularly a man, to the point where he can tell what's going on in your mind ... Do not run after men.

... Love and be faithful to your husband

... Be humble in front of your husband

... When your husband goes to bed, *wai* him at his feet every night without fail. When he has aches and pains, massage him, then you may go to sleep

... Get up before your husband and prepare water for him to wash ...

While your husband is eating, sit and watch him near by so that when he needs something he does not have to raise his voice. Wait until he finishes before you eat.

Unfortunately, or fortunately, depending on your point of view, such slavish devotion is now (and perhaps always was) but a man's dream and a woman's nightmare. However, it remains generally true that the position of women throughout Thai society is one of social and economic inferiority to their men, and they are still frequently referred to as 'the hind legs of the elephant'—which implies that they are just as important as men in terms of economic contribution but that their proper place is at the back, behind their men and supporting them.

This inferiority may not be immediately evident to the visitor, who is likely to come into contact with efficient career women whose pay scale gives them an exceptional amount of independence and status (a top executive secretary, fluent in one or more European languages, a Chinese dialect and possibly with a working knowledge of Japanese can command a salary well above that of a university professor or an army general).

Prostitution

Many male visitors are likely to spend at least part of their leisure time in the company of some of those Thai women who work in one form or another of prostitution. It has been variously estimated that between one and five per cent of the female population pursues this oldest of professions. This means, of course, that at least 95 per cent do not, a simple and obvious point that should be remembered.

The fact that women of easy virtue naturally gravitate around the male visitor's world—where the money is—means that many visitors get an impression of Thai women that is no more true than the impression of western women held by many Thais.

Prostitutes lose face and status, but they also make money, which can eventually rebuy many of the superficial daily actions of respect that are essential to a Thai's mental well-being. While making the money, these girls often compensate psychologically by a brash disregard for Thai norms. Sometimes they almost completely leave the Thai community, while continuing to live in Thailand, and accept only the company of *farang,* Arab or Japanese visitors. Their money provides a certain independence and their behaviour is usually the complete opposite of that advised by Sunthorn Phu.

Propriety

Thai women were probably never enslaved by their men to the same extent as their Indian, Chinese and Japanese sisters, and today many are an obvious success in their profession. But, however successful, broadminded or 'liberated' a woman is, if she walks down the street hand in hand with a man, even if he is her husband, she will lose face. Public displays of affection, common among the playgirls of Bangkok, are not widely accepted. If a woman, Thai or non-Thai, ignores sexual protocol, she is likely to be avoided by other women and approached by men.

All of this has to do with the *public* realm of life; what goes on in *private* is often very different, and none of our business in writing this book! The Thais are quite capable of not seeing what is not made blatantly obvious. Thus the daughter who 'works' in the big city, but continues to send money home, may, when past the age of fancy, retire to her village without too many problems. But *public* impropriety forces people to see, and therefore to react accordingly.

The boundaries of 'impropriety', a changing concept everywhere, in Thailand include any form of physical contact between members of the opposite sex. Even if contact is avoided, it is not really proper for a woman to approach a man directly on an individual basis. It is, for example, the usual practice in Thailand's universities for a female student who needs to see her lecturer in his office to take along a girlfriend, who says nothing and whose only function is to be there.

Taboos on physical contact do not apply between members of the same sex who may, if they wish, walk arm in arm in public without raising any eyebrows. Many western men find this difficult to adjust to. They are not, of course, required to change a lifetime's behaviour, but they should try to understand that the hand on the knee is more an act of friendship than of homosexuality.

Restrictions on social encounter between the sexes present special problems to the non-Thai female visitor, as they do to the Thai professional woman. Social occasions are very often informally segregated into groups of men, usually seated around the alcohol, and groups of women, often structured around the preparation of food. The western wife probably does not want to spend all of her time with the women, and, acknowledging the strange ways of the *farang*, nobody will really mind if she accompanies her husband. Tolerance of *farang* habits does not mean that a Thai male will not be offended if his wife is cornered by Mr West for an unduly long time, even if he is only doing what he thinks is polite by spending some time with the hostess. She will be too polite or embarrassed to break off social contact and her husband is most unlikely to express his displeasure in public. Of course, things are changing among the Thais. Also, many of the functions the visitor attends will be overwhelmingly expat, or at least hosted by expats, in which case norms of the *farang* culture may be more appropriate.

The visitor is largely on his own in deciding how far he can bend or break the rules of sexual interaction in any particular situation. However, he might like to bear in mind that many things may be going on under that phlegmatic Thai exterior and that a large proportion of Thailand's excessively high murder rate is made up of crimes of passion—very often committed some time after the event that germinates them.

If the Thai social scene has lost some of its relaxed atmosphere for the visitor, now intent on avoiding unintended insult, then this is as it should be and as it is for Thais much of the time. The relaxed surface of social encounter is held up by a mild tension of self-conscious aggression avoidance.

Knickers

A minor but pragmatic point about sexual interaction. Taboos against touching across the sex line often extend to undergarments, even when off the body in question. So if your clothes are washed by a man, do not expect him to wash women's undergarments. While being a 'washerboy' involves no more loss of face than being a male cook, washing a woman's knickers would hurt his self-esteem. A female maid may also object to washing a man's underpants, but the ruling seems to be more flexible here.

Chapter Three

RELIGION IN THAILAND

THE WAT

While the visitor's ignorance of Thai norms of courtesy involving one's fellow man will often be excused by the Thai as simply odd, or, at worst, rude, inappropriate behaviour in any religious context will *not* be easily forgiven and deliberate or unintended insult to what the Thais consider sacred could land you in real trouble. Behaving disrespectfully in a Thai temple or to a monk is absolutely taboo.

The Thai Buddhist temple, the *Wat,* can be very simple or extremely elaborate. In small villages the *Wat* may consist only of a simple *Bot* (the central hall of any *Wat,* which shelters the main Buddha image and in which ordinations take place) and a wooden house for one or two monks. In larger population centres, a *Wat* may also include a *Sala,* where laymen gather for social functions, for ceremonies such as the *Sukhwan Nak* (the lay ritual preceding ordination as a monk) and funerals, and even for such secular activity as voting in elections. Somewhere in the *Wat* grounds will be found a *Bo* tree and, to the west of the grounds of the larger temples, a crematorium. In addition, some *Wat* grounds contain a library and one or more *Chedi*, a massive structure usually erected over the bones of a very rich man who wills part of his estate to 'make merit' in this way ('making merit' is considered on page 82).

Some *Wats* in and around Bangkok are so large that they resemble little city states, with roads, paths, housing blocks for hundreds of monks, nuns and lay helpers, and shops and stalls selling refreshments.

A Chedi.

The *Wat* grounds are cut off from the outside world by a wall. This preserves them as quiet, cool and green oases of sanity in the hot and noisy madness of Bangkok. Not surprisingly, *Wat* grounds, in every part of Thailand, provide a place of peaceful recreation, and the *Wat* functions as a community social centre as much as a religious centre.

Women

Women are permitted everywhere, although they should enter the monks' houses only under special circumstances. These houses may be grouped together or dotted around in the forest. No restrictions prevent a menstruating woman from visiting a *Wat*.

Bot

Certain parts of the *Wat* grounds are more sacred than others, the central *Bot* and its Buddha image being the most important. You must take off shoes and hat before entering the *Bot*, usually to the *Sala*, and before entering a monk's quarters. You should also respect the Thai custom of stepping *over* door thresholds, not on them.

Bo Tree

The *Bo* tree, easily recognised by its vast size and sprawling branches (also, it is often clothed in a saffron robe wrapped around its trunk), is sacred because the Buddha attained enlightenment while sitting under one, so please don't allow your children to climb it!

Dress

Normal dress—within the guidelines of Thai respectability we have outlined above—is usually quite acceptable. However, some of the royal *Wat* in Bangkok will refuse entry to women in trousers and men or women in shorts and tee-shirts.

Ambience

The ambience in the *Wat* might surprise the Christian visitor, who is most likely to behave as he would in church. He should remember that Buddhist worship is primarily an individual activity and that people are likely to come and go at any time. Social activity is not clearly distinguished from religious activity and the visitor should not therefore be surprised to find some people, including monks, smoking cigarettes, drinking tea, chewing betel-nuts and quietly chatting during a sermon or ceremony, while others sit in devoted attention. Spittoons are usually placed around on the floor and should be used for saliva, cigarette ash and as general rubbish bins.

Sitting

One problem for the visitor is that very rarely will he find a chair to sit on. High seats, in traditional society, were reserved for royalty, and it remains the norm that most commoners live out their lives sitting, eating and sleeping on the floor.

The most comfortable and healthy way of sitting on the floor is to sit cross-legged and this is the way monks sit. However, it is not the way a layman or a laywoman sits in the *Bot*. There you should sit in the respect position, with the legs tucked under the body, facing the Buddha image. This position is inconvenient and tiring even for Thais and there is no reason why you shouldn't prop yourself up on one arm.

THE MONK

The same sitting position is adopted before monks as before a Buddha image. To sit cross-legged in front of a monk would be to suggest that you are his equal, and you are not.

Status

The superiority of any monk over any layman is very evident in the Thai language which has a set of special vocabulary to be used when

Traditionally, a Buddhist monk wanders with few possessions, living simply, spending his time in meditation, the quest for spiritual knowledge, and teaching the people. Today, monks continue these traditions. Many monks now possess teaching certificates and run simple village schools, bringing education to remote areas.

talking to or about monks. It is also evident in all aspects of monk-layman interaction; laymen eat after, walk behind and seat themselves at a lower level than monks.

There are many obvious reasons, secular and religious, to respect a monk in Thailand. In the villages, many monks continue to fulfil an important secular function by providing basic education to farmers' children and many aid development efforts directly by teaching crafts and trades to the adult population and mobilising cooperative efforts to construct wells, bridges and dams. There are, of course, a few monks in Bangkok and elsewhere who do not keep all of the 227 monastic vows, and a minority who behave in most un-monkish ways, but the vast majority stand as shining examples of virtue in an increasingly unvirtuous world. It is surely healthy that the most respected people in society have taken a vow of poverty, which prevents them eating after noon, and a vow of celibacy, which prevents formation of a priestly caste.

During chantings, the monks sit in a row on a platform that raises them physically above laymen. In one or two of the *Wat* frequented by tourists, the visitor may notice a sign in English saying 'reserved for monks' or 'monks only'; in most places, however, there will be no sign. Even if the monks are not there, you do not sit, or place anything, on this platform. You are welcome to attend chantings and to leave whenever you please, but while you are present do not stand towering over everybody—sit down on the floor.

Abbot

All monks take vows of poverty and humility, but they are as much occupied with relative status within the order as are laymen outside it. Although all monks wear the same 'uniform', individual status is evident in the type of fan carried. The abbot of a large *Wat* is at the top of the local hierarchy and is a powerful man in both religious and secular communities. Nothing should happen within his realm of authority without his knowledge and approval. If you plan to take

A platform raises monks physically above laymen.

photographs, you should ask his permission. (For obvious reasons, this is neither practical nor necessary in those Bangkok *Wat* popular with tourists, where, unless you see a sign forbidding it, you may feel free to take any pictures you wish.) When approaching the abbot, it is not necessary for the visitor to go through the full respect procedure of the triple obeisance, but it is appropriate to lower yourself to beneath his height and give the most respectful *wai*.

Offerings

For those who wish not only to observe but also to *participate,* and make some merit, you may buy in the *Wat,* or take with you, an appropriate set of offerings to the Buddha. The usual offering is three incense sticks (representing the Buddha, his teachings, and the monastic order), some flowers, one candle and a thin piece of gold leaf.

The routine for offering (in Thai, *wai phra*) is not rigidly fixed and you may notice quite an amount of individual variation (although it takes place in public, *wai phra* is essentially a private action between the individual and the Buddha). Usually, the candle is lit first and placed among the other candles in a row set in front of the image and the flowers are placed in water. Then the incense sticks are lit from the candle and held between the palms in a *wai* on the chest. Sitting quietly in the respect position, the Thai would recite in the mind some set phrases in Pali (the language of the Buddhist scriptures), praising the Buddha, his teachings and the order of monks that the Buddha created. This would normally be followed by a wish, expressed mentally in Thai, of a general nature, 'Keep my family healthy,' etc. or a far more specific request, 'Please help me to pass my university exams' or 'Please make me win the lottery this month.' The incense sticks are then stuck into the container of sand provided, the square of gold leaf is pressed onto a Buddha image, and the individual concludes with the triple obeisance. The visitor is quite free to follow this procedure if he wishes, or he may prefer simply to sit in silent communion with his own god.

Offering candles and flowers to the Buddha.

67

Following the simple ritual of *wai phra,* it is normal to donate some money into the box provided. This money goes to the upkeep of the *Wat.* The visitor with religious qualms about engaging in Buddhist ritual may simply put some money in the box (although he cannot escape the merit this action involves!).

If the visitor wishes to present monks with 'presents' and participate even more in Thai life, he should be aware that these objects (usually items of daily need) should be purchased especially for this purpose. You do not simply take some razor blades and toothpaste from the bathroom and give them to the monks; also you do not buy some packets of cigarettes intending to give them to the monks, change your mind, and smoke them yourself.

In the same way, if you choose to make religious merit by offering food, you do not cook up a good meal for yourself and then give a bit to the monks, you feed them first and then eat what remains. Even the flowers you present to the Buddha or the monks should be 'goal specific'. The visitor who innocently sniffs them before offering could find horrible things happening to his nose in the next life!

Meeting Monks

You will encounter monks not just in the *Wat*, but everywhere. Many of them in Bangkok seem to be learning English and almost all of them would be happy to chat with you. Their English is likely to be very textbook and basic.

If a smiling young monk greets you with 'good morning, sir' (it happens all the time!) in much the same way as a doorman at an expensive hotel, please realise that this is purely a linguistic error (nobody has yet produced an English language grammar for such respected people as monks). You may well have a very informal chat with a monk and even exchange addresses, but it is really not done to shake his hand on taking leave. This is the time you can be sure your *wai* is appropriate.

Women

Women present a special problem to monks, who are not supposed even to think about them except in terms of piles of skin and bones. The pile of skin and bones should keep as much social distance between herself and a monk as she possibly can—even if he is her son or fiancé.

Touching of a monk or the robes he is wearing by a woman is absolutely taboo and would involve the monk in elaborate purification rituals. It is also taboo for a woman to hand anything directly to a monk; the object should be passed via a man, set down so that the monk can pick it up, dropped into the monk's bowl or placed on the piece of saffron cloth every monk keeps handy for this purpose.

The visitor should note that monks sit on the back seat of a bus and, for this reason, women avoid this seat. When a crowded Bangkok bus halts to allow a monk to enter, a place will be found for him on this back seat. (No such privilege is accorded the poor nun who must take her chance along with everybody else.) Taking a back seat does not indicate suspension of status. Simply, by using the back door the possibility of brushing past a woman is greatly reduced.

Sacred Being

The presence of a monk on a vehicle, especially one as dangerous as a Bangkok bus, is said to ensure safety. During the 1973 revolution, a group of monks standing up in an open car drove slowly down Rajdamnoen Avenue through the crossfire of police on one side and student revolutionaries on the other and escaped unharmed. The monk is the most sacred of living beings. To kill one, even by accident, is the worst thing you could do in the world.

SACRED SYMBOLS

The most well known of Buddhism's sacred symbols, the one most respected by Thais and, unfortunately, the one most abused by non-Thais (and some Thais) is the Buddha image.

69

Buddha Images

These images are not 'idols'. They do not represent any god and, strictly speaking, are meant only as an aid to help the individual in his path towards the attainment of 'Buddha nature'—the complete elimination of suffering. However, the distinction between worshipping Buddha nature and worshipping the actual image is a fine one and does not change the sacred nature of that image.

It should be needless to say that these images must be treated with the utmost respect. In the past, severe punishments were handed down to anyone guilty of desecrating an image or scraping the gold leaf from its surface. Today, in spite of restrictions on taking images out of the country, they are openly on sale in tourist shops and even set out disrespectfully by the roadside. Many valuable images have disappeared from the country and turned up in museums in the west. These images are stolen by Thais (and if they can't carry the whole image, the normal procedure is just to take the head, since this is the part most valued by the buyer), but often these Thais act in open connivance with otherwise respectable foreign museums and universities.

Such behaviour by a few Thais (unfortunately, those whom the tourist is most likely to encounter) stands in sharp contrast to that of the great majority of the population.

To the average Thai, the Buddha image is not an object of merchandise. It is also not seen primarily as a work of art. In talking about images, special respect language is used, the ordinary term for 'it' is never used and the parts of the image's body are called by those terms used to refer to the King's 'arm', 'head', etc. The Buddha image is an object of veneration, not of decoration. Mistreating a Buddha image in Thailand is tantamount to going into a devout Catholic's house and turning the crucifix upside down.

Even when it comes to sacred images, there are degrees of abuse. Few Thais would object to a non-Thai keeping Buddha images in his home for decoration, as long as these are in a high place (certainly not at foot level). The Thais would also probably hold in their feelings if the visitor entered their home, picked up their image and said, 'How lovely, where can I get one?' (A Thai would *wai* the image before moving or cleaning it.) However, the foreigner would have over-stepped the tolerance line if he climbed onto one of the many huge Buddha images dotted around the country. (The lowest, the feet, being placed upon the highest, the Buddha.)

Some years ago a *farang* family was imprisoned for climbing onto a giant Buddha to pose for a photograph. Their plea that they did not understand Thai conventions and meant no disrespect was dismissed in court.

The King

Next to the Buddha and the monks, the King, although no longer officially 'sacred', is treated with such respect that the visitor might safely categorise him, his family and their images as sacred.

Pictures of the royal family are shown on the screen and the 'King's national anthem' is played before the film in Thai cinemas. If you are on your way in, you stand to attention, arms by your sides. If you are seated, you stand up. Actually, the music played is not the Thai national anthem, but a tune reserved for the presence of the King and Queen or their images; the real national anthem is never played in the cinema. There is also a special tune for when the King's representative is present; the visitor should treat all three tunes with the same respect. And try to remember not to sit down during the pauses, which are part of the music.

Every Thai banknote and coin carries a picture of the King. It is acceptable to fold the notes, put them in your wallet and the wallet in any pocket, even the one you sit on. However, try not to make the same mistake as the poor Frenchman who disagreed with the amount of change given him after paying for his meal in a restaurant. He got into a heated argument and refused to accept the banknotes that the waitress held out for him. He grew so angry that he grabbed the notes, screwed them up, threw them to the floor and ground them underfoot.

His Majesty King Bhumibol Adulyadej during his Coronation (5 May 1950) pronounced the Oath of Accession to the Throne. 'We will reign with righteousness, for the benefit and happiness of the Siamese people.' As he said these words, the King poured ceremonial water symbolising dedication of his whole being to the task of reigning over the Thai nation according to the Moral Principles of the Sovereign.

The King blesses the people at the beginning of Buddhist Lent.

A foot on the King's head! A Thai drinking at a nearby table jumped up, smashed his fist into the Frenchman's surprised face and followed up with a flying kick to the stomach. The limits of tolerance had been passed.

Books

Several other objects of everyday life are not sacred in the same way as the Buddha and the King, but are treated respectfully by Thais. These include books and hats. Books, because until comparatively recently education was confined to the *Wat* (it still is in many remote villages) and the only books were those containing the sacred scriptures. By extension, all books, as vehicles that carry man towards the goal of knowledge and understanding, should be treated appropriately and not defaced. Unfortunately, to judge from the scribblings in books at Chulalongkorn library, this norm of good behaviour requires some social reinforcing.

Hats

Hats are to be treated respectfully because of their association with the head. They should be hung up even if the only place to hang them is a humble nail, not tossed onto the back of a chair. When taking off shoes and hat before entering a *Bot*, do not place your shoes outside the door with your hat resting on top of them because of the unlucky association between feet and head. It is also worth noting that objects of 'low' status should be treated appropriately: placing your shoes on a chair, whether your feet are in them or not, is as bad as placing your hat on the floor.

Elephants and Umbrellas

Many other items carry respect through association with royalty or religion. Rare 'white' elephants are always presented to the King; other elephants work for their living but are regarded as very special animals. Umbrellas have the same association with royalty—the greater the number of tiers, the higher a noble's rank. Ordinary single-tiered umbrellas may, of course, be used to keep off the rain and sun by anybody. But even if there is no rain or sun, an elaborate umbrella will be used to 'shelter' a young man on his way to become a monk, or a dead person on the way to cremation: two moments in existence when a commoner attains his highest status.

Rice

Rice holds a very special position in the hierarchy of animals, plants and objects because it is the giver of life both for the individual and the nation. Most Thais continue to work in the rice fields and rice is still one of Thailand's principal exports.

Rice is said to contain a spiritual essence of its own and every-body, from the King down to the humblest peasant, goes to elaborate lengths to keep the rice spirit happy. Planting and harvesting call for special ceremonies.

Rice dropped on the floor is carefully swept up. Some mothers even rebuke their children, if they complain of tummy-ache after overeating, that they are insulting the rice goddess. If the rice goddess is insulted, the rice crop will suffer. As long as the rice goddess is happy, the Thais will eat. So please don't throw your leftover rice down the toilet.

Chapter Four

THAI WAYS OF SEEING

If the Thai world could be fully pressed between the covers of a book, it probably would not be worth reading. Our task in this part of the book is not to provide the complete picture of this fascinating jigsaw puzzle called Thailand. That would be impossible because the pieces of the puzzle are changing all the time. We limit ourselves to considering those pieces which most intrigue, worry and please the visitor unfamiliar with Thai ways of seeing and doing. When the visitor understands something of Thai ways of seeing things, he will have learnt a lot about Thailand and a great deal about himself.

THE KING AND THE PEASANT

In searching, unsuccessfully, for a nutshell to put Thailand into, we came across a Thai folktale which sums up something of the Thai way of seeing things. In this tale a king meets a peasant and asks what he does with his surplus.

The peasant replies:

> Your Majesty, all the money I am able to save, after paying the expenses of our frugal household, I divide into four parts. The first I bury in the ground; the second I use to pay my creditors; the third I fling into the river; and the fourth and last part I give to my enemy.

The king asks the peasant to explain his strange behaviour and is told:

> The money I bury in the ground is the money I spend on alms and in making merit. The money I give to my creditors is what it costs me to keep my father and mother, to whom I owe everything I have. The money I fling into the river is the money I spend on gambling and drink and opium; and the money I give to my enemy is the money I give to my wife.

(translated by A. Le May,
Siamese Tales Old and New, London, 1930)

The peasant spends his money on four things: religion, parents, enjoyment and wife. His views on supporting parents and wife are diametrically opposed. The remainder of his money is divided between the temporary pleasures of life and the permanent treasure of Buddhism. An investment in religion is the only insurance for the future.

This ancient tale remains a favourite with modern Thais. Things have not changed too much.

LIFE

We asked a group of monks to try and express the essential truth of Buddhism in one sentence. They unanimously agreed on 'all life is suffering'. They were sitting in front of a wooden wall on which somebody had written, in English, 'Life is very fun why quickly to go.' All Thais know that life is suffering, and almost all Thais seem to enjoy life to the full. If there is a contradiction in this, the Thais are not worried by it.

The Five Basic Precepts

The five great commandments of Buddhism are as follows:
1. Do not take life.
2. Do not steal.
3. Do not commit adultery.
4. Do not tell untruths.
5. Refrain from intoxicants.

All Thais know these commandments, almost all Thais are Buddhists, Thailand is one of the most Buddhist countries in the world, and yet a great many Thais break most or all of these commandments almost every day.

Taking Life

Few Thais deliberately take life, but all Thais love to eat. Almost all Thai food contains pieces of meat, usually pork, chicken or fish. Even the monks eat meat. Eating meat requires the killing of animals. It also requires some very Thai rationalisations which permit full indulgence yet leave the commanding principle intact. Monks explain that they eat meat because they must eat anything put in their bowls with neither enjoyment nor disgust; one famous monk is said to have calmly eaten a leper's thumb that fell into the bowl! Laymen resort to less convincing excuses, 'I just took the fish out of the water and it died without killing,' 'the chicken was already dead when I bought it,'

Almost all Thais seem to enjoy life to the full. The visitor should be prepared to accept an occasional lapse in polite behaviour at festival time.

and even 'the pig was fulfilling its destiny, that's why it was born a pig'. Fortunately, very few Thai Buddhists find themselves in a position where they would have to take life since most are rice farmers and slaughter-men are mostly non-Buddhists.

Theft

Most Thais do not steal; the minority do. Unfortunately, the minority seem to be quite active and Thailand has one of the highest crime rates in the world. *Khamoys* (thieves) abound. Any bus, even in the centre of Bangkok, is a target for the *khamoy*, who enters through the back door with knife or gun, grabs what wallets and gold chains he can, exits through the front onto his friend's motorcycle and flees the scene. Houses and pedestrians are also fair game.

79

Apart from the professional *khamoys*, many Thais employ a 'fish out of water' rationale for keeping what is found—'It fell off the back of a truck.' Considering the number of things that really do fall off the backs of trucks, the explanation is reasonable. The practice of finders-keepers might be considered fair compensation for Thais who live in constant knowledge that any day home and family could be smashed to smithereens by a ten-ton truck.

Cheating

More subtle forms of *khamoy*ery are performed on hapless visitors by those shopkeepers who sell jewellery constituting 50 per cent of the stated gold and silver value and which would be much cheaper back home. If you are staying some time in the country, make the fact known and you may get a better deal. This is because any reputable disreputable jeweller will give a guarantee of full refund if goods are found to be of less than stated quality. This guarantee is worth the paper it is written on and little more, unless you have several months to waste in legal inactivities. Not all jewellers are dishonest, but visitors should note that several laboratories will test gold, silver and gems for a small fee and that this service is provided to fulfil a need.

Cheating can have its charming side. At the Ban Chieng archaeological site a beautiful old lady offered us a 'genuine Buddhist monk's bowl guaranteed over 6000 years old' (the Buddhist era began 543 years before the birth of Christ).

Sex

The third precept—to refrain from adultery—is kept publicly and often broken privately. The visitor may notice that many of the middle-range hotels not only have the strange habit of renting rooms by the hour, but also have very quaint basement 'car parks'. As every car pulls in, a young boy runs to pull a curtain and hide the car from the world. The purpose of this roof-to-ground curtain is not to keep the car clean.

Telling the Truth

The fourth commandment is very difficult to keep in daily life. Truth and untruth are, of course, relative and debatable concepts. The Thai does not deliberately lie, but also does not deliberately tell the truth. Norms of respect and politeness require flattery and exaggeration.

Thais are masters of the 'sideways lie'—stepping aside from any possible unpleasantness by saying whatever is required. Sometimes, however, in circumstances when the westerner would white-lie, Thais can be embarrassingly candid, as we found out one night at the Bangkok Alliance Française, where we were treated to a superb exhibition of flattery and candour.

The Thai master of ceremonies stood on the stage for ten minutes, lauding, in textbook French, the praises of the film star he was to introduce to a packed audience. Having stretched the peak of flattery into a seemingly endless ridge, he finally came to '… and it is with the deepest honour that I am privileged to present to you the one and only Xxx.' Silence. Xxx did not rush up and shake the outstretched hand. More silence. Until at last the monsieur whispered in Thai to a waiting auditorium, 'Where is Xxx?' A Thai doorkeeper answered clear and loud from the back of the hall, *'pai hong nam'*—'in the toilet'.

Intoxicants

The fifth commandment is openly broken. Alcoholism is a problem and although the sales of the two major brands of Thai whisky, Mekhong and Sang Som, report a 20 per cent drop in sales during the three-month Buddhist Lent, few Thais consider drinking alcohol to be particularly unBuddhist.

Other intoxicants include marijuana, opium and heroin, all of which, although illegal, are produced and consumed in a quantity great enough to give Thailand one of the largest drug addiction problems in the world. Production and sale has been restricted in recent years and visitors are warned that many foreigners are in Thai prisons because of drug related offences.

Ideal and Reality

Daily contravention of the five basic Buddhist precepts places them very much in the realm of the ideal, that which should be rather than that which is. Every society has contradictions between ideal and reality. Western societies could no more be adequately described by reference to the Ten Commandments of the Old Testament, than could the behaviour and feelings of most Thais be expressed by reference to Buddhist precepts.

Making Merit

The Thai does not *seem* to have any great problems living with his contradictions. This is perhaps because of other aspects of Thai Buddhist philosophy which teach that the individual is responsible for his own destiny and that he can change that destiny for the better by accumulating religious merit. Religious merit is gained by keeping the precepts but also by other actions which may be easier and much more fun.

Merit-making in everyday life often means little more than giving money, or things bought with money, to the *Wat* and its monks. This refers us back to the Thai folktale mentioned at the beginning of this chapter in which the peasant balances the amount spent on daily pleasures with the amount spent on merit-making activities. Most Thais seem happy to strike a balance. Just how effective this balance is in bridging the gulf between ideal and reality is uncertain. However, the idea of balance is essential to any understanding of Thai personality and behaviour.

FAMILY

The family is the first world. A safe world. A world which is, for the first few years at least, gentle, kind and good. It is the world in which an individual learns to obey and respect his elders and betters. The family makes a Thai.

Rules of Respect

The child quickly learns that by behaving in a way that openly demonstrates consideration for the feelings of others, obedience, humility, politeness and respect, he can make people like him and be nice to him. This behaviour may be summed up in one Thai word, *krengjai*.

Krengjai is usually translated as 'consideration'. It is more than that. It is a feeling. A father might consider the welfare of his children but he would not feel *krengjai* towards them. His children, in considering his feelings and adjusting their behaviour to give him peace of mind, do feel *krengjai*. *Krengjai* is felt by the person who considers. In Thailand the person 'who considers' is normally the inferior in any social relationship. Thus, *krengjai* has a lot to do with the hierarchical Thai system of status and respect.

Rules of respect, strongest in the relationship between children and parents, are also very evident between children. The younger should obey the elder, the elder is responsible for the behaviour of the younger.

Terms used between family members are often extended to the Thai community, a practice which indicates relative hierarchical status rather than the establishment of close, family-type relationships. A *phii* (elder brother or sister) is always superior to a *nong*. A *nong* could be a close friend or a complete stranger filling up the car petrol tank or waiting on tables. Even husbands and wives use *phii* or *nong* to refer to each other, and they are, of course, very unlikely to be brother and sister.

In the same way, *luang poh*, *luang ta* and *luang phii* ('father', 'grandfather' and 'elder brother' with the respect prefix *luang*) may be used to refer to monks, *poh luang* is used in parts of Thailand to refer to the village headman, *mae chi* ('mother nun') refers to nuns and *mae khrua* ('mother kitchen') is used with a female cook. 'Uncles', 'aunts' and 'cousins' may have no biological relationship at all.

Luang poh. A monk continues the tradition of teaching the young.

Social and Economic Unity

The Thai village household is, by Asian standards, quite small, and is usually confined to a couple, two or three children and perhaps an aging parent, aunt or uncle. Houses vary between the strongly built, ornately carved, large houses of the wealthy and the frail bamboo boxes of the poor. Differences are much greater in town. Large, modern villas, with servants to run and open the gate at the master's tooting car horn and shacks of cardboard and tin exist side by side.

Rural Thai families continue the long tradition of social and economic unity. Young children do household chores and look after younger brothers and sisters, older children help their parents in the family rice fields.

Urban families lose the unity that comes from working together. However, low wages mean that all family members must contribute to family costs. In Thailand, 'housewives' are found only in privileged households. Wives and children of poor families in the city make cakes, thread flowers into garlands, recycle waste paper into paper bags, sell newspapers and flowers to car owners caught in traffic jams, or do one or more of the thousand jobs that support Bangkok's 'informal economy'.

Security

The family traditionally provided an individual with security against sickness and old age. This remains true in most cases, but in towns, an increasing number of old people find themselves spending their last years in the *Wat* or in the anonymous and alien environment of an institution.

CHILDREN

The Unlucky Minority

The Thai reputation for pampering small children is well deserved. Unfortunately, it is tarnished by the media exposure of the fact that each year thousands of children are left in temple grounds, where they are often raised by the monks and nuns, or abandoned in the street to be raised in orphanages. Newspapers frequently report a flourishing trade in child labour. Parents in town with no means of support and very poor parents in the villages may sell their child for one or two years to 'agents' in exchange for a few sacks of rice. These children are often set to work long hours in factories with guards at the door to prevent them leaving. Occasionally some are rescued in muchpublicised police raids, but most grow up in an environment that is cruel and depressing by any standards and, in later life, enter the world as *khamoys*, pimps and prostitutes.

The Lucky Majority

The unfortunate lot of the unlucky minority must be placed in perspective. Most Thai children are not sold into semi-slavery. On the contrary they are pampered and fussed over for the first few years of life. Studies of Thai child-rearing patterns suggest that this produces a pleasant, gentle personality but also tends to kill initiative and retard the development of an inquiring mind.

We are none too sure of this process of cause and effect. We are sure, however, that most young children are treated extraordinarily well. The visitor will see adults on a Bangkok bus giving up their seats for children; western children are told to give up their seats for adults.

Avoiding Aggression

Such pampering does not last for long and all too soon children are hard at work. If early childhood teaches self-indulgence, late child-hood teaches self-sufficiency and responsibility. The adolescent Thai personality is often a mixture of these conflicting patterns of socialisation. An individual may provide for himself and sometimes for others, yet is never encouraged, as the western child is, to 'stand on his own feet'. The Thai learns how to avoid aggression rather than how to defend himself against it. If children fight, even in defence, they are usually punished. The only way to stay out of trouble is to flee the scene.

The Monsters

Some of the most horrible children in Thailand belong to expat families living in the country on a temporary or permanent basis.

The expat child is likely to be bigger, stronger, better nourished and psychologically much more prepared to compete, defend and win than are the Thai children he is playing with. Some, but not all, expat children become impossibly pretentious and arrogant. They are aware of the Thai respect status system but are outside it and, in a sense, above it. Their hands are not brought together in a *wai* when an adult

The lucky majority.

visitor enters the house, as are those of Thai children. The Thai adults of the expat child's world are usually servants who will spoil him to keep him quiet.

One Thai father told us he felt sorry for his boss (an American) who had a *luk nerakhun*—an ungrateful son. Urged, unwillingly, to explain how he had come to this conclusion, he said that he had visited the boss's house and heard him *ask* (and not *tell*) his son to clean the car. The son had grumbled but finally agreed to do the job when his father *paid* him. Some visitors to Thailand think a Thai will do anything for money. This Thai suggested that payment between a father and son was tantamount to denying a kinship link.

'Huh!' says the expat reader. 'My children must be prepared to live in their society, not in Thai society.' We agree. And having pointed out the problem, we offer no solution. To encapsulate them in an expats-only situation might produce even more arrogant monsters and would deny children the unique opportunity to understand

Thais and learn the Thai language without tears. We would suggest only that parents be aware that their pride and joy may be another child's hate and misery.

AUTHORITY

The Thai child's world expands as he grows up and very soon it includes far more people than the members of his immediate family. In an agricultural setting, *krengjai* feelings and behaviour would expand as this world grows. All elders would receive something of the consideration and respect an individual demonstrates for his father and mother.

Strangers

There comes a point in life when an individual needs to interact with people who are not family, neighbours, friends or even fellow villagers. He enters the world of strangers: the schoolteacher, policeman, *kamnan* (the head of a *tambon*, subdistrict, composed of 10–20 villages), *nai amphur* (district officer) and people who come in trucks and show movies on a big screen which they set up in the grounds of the *Wat* and then talk about strange things or line a child up with all the other frightened children and stick needles in his arms, poke sticks down his throat and tell him to say *aaaaaarrrh*.

This unknown world is potentially dangerous. It wants to be obeyed and insists on being obeyed. So, the most sensible way to deal with it is for the individual to behave in a way that obviously demonstrates obedience, humility, politeness and respect; to behave, superficially at least, in the way he would behave in front of worshipful parents, and hope that this will make strangers like him and be nice to him.

By extending *krengjai* behaviour to the outside world, the potential dangers involved in temporary, unknown and unpredictable relationships are, hopefully, neutralised.

Fear

If, in spite of conforming to all respect procedures, the stranger (or the father!) does not respond with kindness, but becomes hostile, the individual's external actions (the superficial world on view) remain the same, and humility may even be exaggerated to the point a western observer might call degradation. *Inside*, however, things have changed. The feeling of *krengjai* (consideration/respect) has changed to *krengklua*, literally 'fear'.

At this point the most sensible thing for the individual to do is to get out of the situation as fast as he can before nasty things happen. Sometimes, the individual may literally flee the scene. More usual is to say and promise anything to placate this unreasonable force and, at the first opportunity, to break off social contact and make sure it is never renewed in the future.

Humiliation

If the individual is impossibly stuck in a *krengklua* situation, self-degradation will continue to the point where wild violence erupts. A wife continuously beaten, a civil servant humiliated once too often, a servant treated too contemptuously; all could eventually rebel, delaying urgent letters, adding a few zeros in the accounts, planting some drugs in a compromising place, or even running amok with a meat cleaver or hiring a thug to kill or maim.

EQUALITY

Few Thais are equal and many are more unequal than others. Twins born minutes apart and raised in the same family will still refer to each other in *phii/nong* terms. A man 34 years 29 days 5 hours 4 minutes and 3 seconds old is the elder of a man 34 years 29 days 5 hours 4 minutes and 2.9 seconds old. Other things being equal, the *phii* (elder) is superior. Of course, other things rarely are equal, but a surprising number of Thais can tell you, within the margins of accuracy of their father's clock, precisely when they were born.

Were each Thai midwife equipped with a stopwatch, it should be possible to rank the entire population from one to 55 million in terms of the age criteria. If it were possible to place an equally exact numerical value on all other attributes of status, add up each individual's totals, and arrange individuals in perfect pecking order, all social behaviour in any situation would be perfectly predictable. The anthropologist's dream and nightmare.

Seniority

Status and seniority are so much parts of Thai life, Thais rarely give them a second thought. The single file of monks on the morning almsround walks in abstract detachment from such worldly considerations as status and prestige—the senior monk at the front and the junior at the rear. The guests at a wedding, retirement, funeral and other ceremonies are pleasant, polite and *wai* each other at the same time (almost) and at the same height (almost), before lining up to bless the centre of attraction in order of status. It seems to happen naturally.

No caste marks, no secret signs, everybody dressed more or less the same. The hierarchy is not perfect and there are areas of overlap, but surprisingly few. How do they know? How do they do it? And why? Few Thais would be able to tell you. A historian could give you some idea.

Walking in abstract detachment from such worldly considerations as status and prestige, the senior monk at the front and the junior monk at the rear.

King Trailok

It all started at a time when westerners outside the Holy Roman Empire were still painting themselves blue and living in caves. A long time ago. We will drag the reader back only to the mid-15th century to the time of King Paramatrailokanatha, whose name is usually shortened by Thais, for obvious reasons, to Trailok.

King Trailok, seeking to establish the basis for a peaceful kingdom, slotted together Hindu and Confucianist ideas, added some Thai interpretation, and came up with the *saktina* system. This political, social and religious hierarchy was to continue with only slight modifications until the sweeping reforms introduced by King Chulalongkorn (1868–1910) and the abolition of the Divine Kingship which followed the revolution of 1932. Centuries of intense social rigidity are not easy to reform, however, and the ghost of *saktina* continues to influence everyday Thai social relationships.

King Trailok, lacking computers and other paraphernalia of a modern totalitarian state, sought to control feuding feudal lords by setting each to compete peacefully with all others for the King's favours. Recognising that the amount of land a man held was the key to wealth, status and power, King Trailok rationalised individual landholdings so that no man posed a threat to the Kingship, yet all men were able to increase their holdings and power through royal patronage.

Saktina Gradings

Each landowner was accorded a number which corresponded to the amount of land held. This number was called *saktina*, literally power of the fields.

The top officials, the *Chao Phya*, held a grading of 10,000 and were allowed a maximum 4000 acres of land. Commoners, on the other hand, unless they had some special merits, held a *saktina* grading of 20 and could own up to 10 acres (8 are sufficient to support a family of 4–6 in comfort).

A man's first or major wife (*mia luang*) held half the *saktina* grading of her husband, the minor wife (*mia noy*) held one quarter, and a slave wife held no grading but became a *mia noy* upon bearing her husband's child. The numbers have gone but, some would argue, the position of women has not changed much since the time of King Trailok.

If a man were to be fined, the fine would relate to his *saktina*. If a man were to be compensated, he received an amount in accordance with his *saktina*. *Saktina* permeated all economic, legal and social life and determined all deferential behaviour. A *saktina* of 1000 meeting a *saktina* of 1500 would *wai* first.

Brilliant in its simplicity, the system was not really adaptable to bank managers, noodle sellers and long-nosed, redheaded merchants from strange lands. It also didn't help very much in promoting Thailand's international image as 'the land of the free'. It was therefore officially abolished, along with slavery, in 1905 by King Chulalongkorn.

King Chulalongkorn

King Chulalongkorn was perhaps the most revolutionary Thai who ever lived. He began his amazing rule by abolishing the obeisance laws which kept commoner heads below royal feet. By that time he had already introduced Thailand's first western-style school, with an English headmaster, in the Grand Palace. He went on to promote the spread of secular schooling throughout the Kingdom and is today known as the 'father of modern education' and the founder of modern Thailand. The King who did most to desanctify the Kingship is today one of the most revered of all Thai Kings. The anniversary of his death is a national holiday and on that day the visitor will see students and civil servants stretching out in obeisance to his statue on Rajdamnoen Nok Avenue. This statue has become the centre of weekly urban cult gatherings, at which thousands of Thais of all classes pay homage and make vows to the father of the nation.

Students and civil servants pay annual obeisance to the memory of King Chulalongkorn.

King Chulalongkorn is usually accredited with having kept Thailand free when every other Southeast Asian state was collapsing to the forces of colonialism. The threat from outside required rapid modernisation of the armed forces and the bureaucracy and King Chulalongkorn had the foresight and abilities to instigate and carry this through.

He also had some personal reasons for modernising the Kingship. One of the most tragic ironies of Thai history is the death of Chulalongkorn's Queen Consort and daughter, which resulted directly from regulations which were designed to segregate and protect royalty.

The Queen Consort Sunanda-Kumariratn died on a quiet waterway just a few metres from many devoted subjects. To explain why, we reproduce from H. G. Quaritch-Wales' great work on Thai royalty, *Siamese State Ceremonies*, a translation of the regulations existing at the time of the tragedy. More than anything else, this quotation sums up the historical relationship between king and commoner.

If a boat founders, the boatmen must swim away; if they remain near the boat they are to be executed. If the boat founders and the royal person falls into the water and is about to drown, let the boatmen stretch out the signal-spear and throw the coconuts so that he may grasp them if he can. If he cannot, they may let him seize the signal-spear. If they lay hold of him to rescue him, they are to be executed. He who throws the coconuts is to be rewarded with forty ticals of silver and one gold basin. If the barge sinks and someone else sees the coconuts thrown and goes to save the royal person, the punishment is double and all his family is to be exterminated. If the barge founders and someone throws the coconuts so that they float towards the shore (i.e., away from the royal person), his throat is to be cut and his home confiscated.

So extensive was Chulalongkorn's modernisation that European observers in the 1870s voted Thailand the Asian country most likely to industrialise. (The same observers thought Japan unlikely to succeed!)

King Bhumibol

Today, commoners may stand in the presence of the King and even snap his photograph. King Bhumibol (this is the usual English spelling; Thais pronounce the name *Phumiphon*, *ph* = a breathy English *p*) came to the throne in 1946 and has consistently built on the heritage of King Chulalongkorn.

Visitors who tend to see monarchies as relics of feudal times will be pleasantly surprised to find King Bhumibol very much a man of the 20th century. Far from being the cloistered monarch of the past, the Thai King of today covers an average of 50,000 kilometres a year, much of it in jeeps he drives himself, visiting the people in the most dangerous and remote parts of the Kingdom. He also initiates and leads development programmes and conducts experiments in Chitrlada Palace designed to provide renewable energy resources.

King Bhumibol. Very much a modern monarch.

Few long-term visitors to Thailand leave without developing a deep respect for the Thai King. A man of many talents, the Thai King must surely be the only monarch in the world to play both the saxophone and the clarinet and have a recording of jazz compositions in the shops. Like King Chulalongkorn, King Bhumibol has been granted the title "The Great."

The most respected people in Thailand are those who have dedicated themselves to the pursuit of the spiritual and material ideal of overcoming suffering.

Centuries of Respect

Things have changed a lot in Thailand, as everywhere, but old habits change slowly in a predominantly agricultural society. Most Thais continue to think of the Royal Family as something more than flesh and blood, and land continues to be the major source of wealth, power and status. Equality in the sense of equal shares and equal status is an ideal yet to be realised in both the East and the West. Thais respect the ideal and are moving slowly towards it while managing to steer clear of much of the senseless bloodshed and suffering that result from forcing the pace.

Much of the charm of the Thai people, the *wai*, the smile, the consideration for the comfort of others, is a result of centuries of respect between non-equals. The visitor should try to remember that the most respected people in this country are those who have dedicated themselves to the pursuit of the spiritual and material ideal of overcoming suffering. Thais do not seek to gain the world, but they do wish to keep their soul.

STATUS

Thais are held together by being held apart. This is the basis of the Thai status system which permits individuals to pursue their own development while providing a social framework for national identity and common prosperity.

Structure

Thai society is stratified in an individual way that may confuse the western visitor used to simple upper/middle/working class distinctions. The complexity, and individuality, of the Thai system will be revealed if you begin the daunting task of learning Thai. Then you will be intrigued by the ease with which a Thai changes language and behaviour patterns, slipping in and out of positions of superior, inferior and equal.

Visitors from most non-English-speaking European countries will be used to manipulating two words for 'you'. In modern Europe 'inferior you' is decreasingly heard and may cause offence. Not so in Thailand. The Thai adjusts all of his language to suit the social situation. We give the 'status chart' (opposite) for the personal pronouns 'I' and 'you' only to indicate the complexity of the Thai deference system. On this chart alone there are eleven different words for 'you'. The chart is adapted from the one given at the very end of the AUA intensive 20-week Thai course—some Thais consider it an over-simplification!

Some people are very evidently at the top of the structure. The King, Royal Family and monks (and Buddha images) are all *phra* (excellent). They are excellent in every sense and stand as moral custodians of the Thai world. Almost every Thai household has Buddha images, pictures of monks and many pictures of the King and

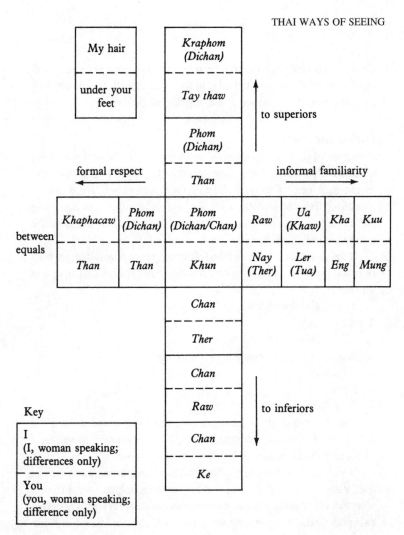

Status chart. The central box indicates safe respectful neutrality when speaking to strangers whose status is not evident or to dangerous inferiors, e.g. drunks and traffic policemen.

Queen. The Thai world is simply inconceivable without these essential components. An individual status system must have a commonly agreed point of excellence at the very top of the system.

Guess the Status

For those of us who fall short of perfection, and whose status is not immediately evident, there is the deceptively simple Thai 'small talk' to put each one of us in his place. Thus, outside of 'fixed status' situations like restaurants, taxi-cabs, etc, where the customer buys higher status, first encounters establish as quickly as possible the relative standing of the individuals involved.

If the visitor bears in mind the following seven points it might help him in this subtle game of guess-the-status. A Thai is likely to assess you on the following:
1. Superficial appearance
2. Age
3. Occupation
4. Wage and (intra-organisation) ranking
5. Education
6. Family
7. Social connections

The last two of these points are the most important and tend to determine appearance, occupation, wage and education. Most really important Thais are recognisable by their surname.

Because surnames were introduced as a legal requirement only in the 1920s, when each family had to pick a name that was different from any other name in the Kingdom, you can be sure (with one or two exceptions) that people with the same surname are related in some way.

Titles

Top families in the 1920s were given their surnames by the King and most top families then are top families now. It would be a simple exercise to list the 'top hundred', but we refrain from doing so! The visitor may be guided, however, by the fact that a great many important people have titles: royal, civil service or military.

A surprising number of people in top positions have royal titles; these decrease in status and scarcity following a five-generation rule. The visitor should be aware of this ruling since any title is inevitably displayed in abbreviated form on namecards and invitations and provides an instant guide to status. These titles with their English abbreviations are as follows:

P.O.C.   *Phra Ong Chao*, grandchild of King
M.C.   *Mom Chao*, child of P.O.C.
M.R.   *Mom Rajawong*, child of M.C.
M.L.   *Mom Luang*, child or wife of M.R. and wife of M.C.

With the fifth generation, the title is lost. The King and Queen, Crown Prince and the Princesses stand in a category above all these ranks. They do not, of course, hand out namecards.

Apart from royal titles, you might come across some other titles which do not show royal descent. Civil service titles have not been granted since 1932 but are still frequently heard among older members of 'society'. These are, in descending order:

Chao Phya (wife: *Khun Ying*)
Phya
Phra
Luang
Khun (spelt and pronounced differently in Thai from *Khun* meaning 'you' or 'Mr')

If somebody has a title, use it in place of 'you', 'he' or 'her' when talking to them or about them. You may like to follow the same practice with high military rankings, which are probably more important in Thailand than they are back home because Prime Ministers, and other very important people, have a strong tendency to be top army personnel. These rankings are translated into the nearest American equivalent on the English side of the namecard and are therefore not given here.

Knowing One's Place

The visitor might notice that the who-do-you-know game is not limited to top Thais. Establishing social contacts with people of standing is the aim of all middle-class Thais, who compete among themselves to curry favour with the powerful in much the same way as people did in the *saktina* days.

Anthropologists have noted that Australian aborigines who meet on walkabout sit down and go through their family trees until they find an ancestor they share. This common point in the past provides the basis for cooperation and interaction in the present. Versions of the same process of placing strangers exist in all cultures, particularly in Asia and especially in Thailand. (And, we might add, most of all within expat communities!)

The main purpose of the status game, for most Thais, is not one-upmanship or social advance. On the contrary, the game is a part of knowing one's place and behaving accordingly. However, even when relative statuses are clearly evident, conversations between strangers have a strong tendency to follow the pattern established by the status game. The man who cuts your hair, the girl who sells you a packet of aspirin, the boy who brings you a Coca-Cola; they are all inferiors, they know it and you know it, but they still ask the same personal questions. In such situations, the purpose of the game is not really to establish relative status but rather to flatter the superior.

The visitor who begins to learn some Thai will very quickly pick up the pattern, since everybody is a stranger. If you can say nothing else, you will soon be able to give name, age, marital status, occupation, wage, reason for coming to Thailand, and the price of your new blue jeans in something approaching understandable Thai.

SUCCESS

When we asked ordinary Thais (the non-VIPs) the simple question, 'How do you measure success?' we received a variety of answers. 'If I'm still alive at the end of the day' (grinning *tuk-tuk* driver). 'Five hundred baht a day' (lottery ticket seller). 'Money, lots of it' (shopkeeper, office-worker, policeman). 'Being a policeman' (schoolboy). 'Having lots of friends' (schoolgirl). 'Marrying a rich *farang* and going to America' (hotel waitress). 'More of things' (rice farmer). Most answers were personal and subjective, involved money, were within the realm of possibility and emphasised immediacy and luck.

Success, for most people, is a day-to-day affair. Very few could imagine themselves moving up the social ladder and surprisingly few expressed their view of 'success' in a religious way, although almost everybody subsequently said that monks and royalty were the people they most respected. While few men can obtain a royal title, almost all can ordain and achieve the pinnacle of respect during their period as a monk. About 50 per cent or more Thai males do enter the monkhood, but most remain for only the three-month period of *Phansa* (Buddhist Lent). Above the multitude of 'ordinary' people stands a comparatively small, extremely well educated and very 'successful' élite whose members fill the top echelons of the military and the civil service.

103

Paths to Success

The typical top government servant comes from a socially acceptable family. He would receive his first degree in an arts subject from Chulalongkorn or Thammasat universities in Bangkok and take an M.A. overseas, probably in America. Upon return from abroad he would ordain as a monk for three months, marry wisely, enter government service and prove himself loyal to a 'patron', often a friend of the family, who would take the protégé under his wing and repay obedience and loyalty by recommending promotion within the service.

Today not everybody with a good education can be sure of a top position in the civil service, which is markedly 'top heavy', and many graduates now reply to advertisements in the English language press for managerial positions in large multinational companies. These advertisements often stipulate the Chulalongkorn/Thammasat/overseas university qualification, always require a high level of competence in English and, for top positions, often state that candidates must have 'good social connections'. The reason for this last qualification is that the Thai manager, if he is to secure advantages for his non-Thai company, must be of recognised status and able to operate within the traditional framework of Thai social interaction. In this way, the successful Thai, although he may work for an international company, reinforces traditional Thai social structure.

Thais throughout the status hierarchy resist dreaming of the impossible and tend to think of success either in day-to-day terms ('cook only for today') or as something that comes from consistently staying out of trouble and thereby pleasing everybody. All agree that 'success' means more of what they have not got enough of, usually money.

CHANCE

The philosophy of *karma*, that good and bad things happen to an individual as a consequence of his good and bad actions in this and past lives and the Thai inclination for present indulgence rather than long-term investment, provide the socio-economic base for the major Thai industries of gambling and fortune-telling.

Gambling

In Thailand it is difficult to resist the temptation to gamble. National lottery tickets are on sale on every corner, each bus ticket contains a lottery number and even conscription into national service is determined by the luck of the draw, a black ticket and you are off the hook, a red one and in you go. Even the poorest paid workers periodically get together (especially after pay-day) to put a few baht each into a kitty and play a game of pure chance to allow one or two of them to go on a temporary binge of indulgence. Not to take part might be seen as anti-social.

Gambling, unless officially organised is illegal but laws are not strictly enforced. For most people it provides a relatively cheap form of entertainment, is a favourite topic of conversation and, since winners inevitably treat their friends, provides endless opportunities for getting together and having a good time. Some forms of gambling, cock-fighting, fish-fighting and betting on the outcome of a Thai boxing bout, not only provide entertainment but also involve high degrees of skill and can become full-time occupations.

The average Thai spends as much on gambling as he does on religious activity, and the second expense is often directly related to the first. Some people *tham boon* (give food and other items of daily use to the monks) and then immediately ask a monk to give them two numbers; they later match these with the final two numbers on a lottery ticket before buying it. Others prefer a less overt but more direct request to the source of all knowledge and during the quiet moment of *wai phra* (offering flowers, incense and a prayer to the Buddha) will follow the set recitation with a request for a modest win in the next lottery.

A Chinese-Thai spirit medium demonstrates that he has the protection of an important guardian spirit.

Changing the Future

Frequently, Thais try to bribe the gods and spirits, offering to reward extra-human assistance if they are successful in a bet, an examination, request for promotion, job application, a courtship or in recovering from an illness, all things which involve an element of chance. The major part of the bribe is paid only after success has been achieved (as in the material world!). Not to keep such promises would be very dangerous.

One favourite object of votive behaviour in Bangkok is the elephant god at the Erawan corner. This shrine is constantly covered with mounds of flowers and a professional group of musicians and dancers in classical costumes earn a good income from a stream of people who fulfil vows by hiring their services for a fixed period of time to play and dance for the god.

In fulfilment of a vow, a walk through the fire pit in a Chinese temple.

In almost every *Wat* there is a monk to tell fortunes. Many laymen and women also engage in this activity. For some, this simply involves reading cards and hands and rewards are small. For others, however, fortune-telling and manipulation of destiny can be a highly lucrative, if dangerous, profession. To prove real communication with the spirit world, a *khon song* needs to do more than simply go into a trance. The highest paid will demonstrate their powers periodically, often in contest with colleagues of the profession, by walking across fire, cutting the tongue or sticking knives and skewers through various parts of the body. Having demonstrated that he or she has the protection of an important guardian spirit, the spirit medium does not merely tell your fortune but may actively intervene in it, by enlisting the help of his familiar to solve your personal problems or satisfy your wishes. All, of course, for an appropriate fee.

Intervention in individual destiny by a spirit medium or spirit doctor is usually specific and short-term. It should always be accompanied by a more long-term balancing of individual *karma* through making religious merit, the only sure path to a brighter future.

TIME

While sitting for a day at the immigration office to get a visa extension, watching sleepy fingers slowly tap-tap-have-a-smoke-tap-tap a dozen forms, or waiting for a secretary to come back from her two-hour lunch break, the visitor might reflect on the surprising fact that one thing Thai and English have in common is the saying 'time is money'.

Punctuality

When necessary (in the context of Thai values), Thais can be extremely punctual. They will get married at a time set by an astrologer within an auspicious few minutes and note the precise time of a child's birth for his future use in fortune-telling. They can also move extremely quickly, as anybody who has travelled from Bangkok to Chiengmai by bus will verify.

For most of the time, however, such punctuality is unnecessary, especially in the agricultural world where people get up at dawn, move off to the fields and stay there until the work is done, which may take two hours or may take ten, depending on the stage in the rice cycle. For these people, the traditional distinctions made in the Thai language are quite enough: dawn, morning, late morning, noontime, afternoon until about 4 p.m., early evening (4–6 p.m.), night (7–12 p.m.), and nightguard (midnight–dawn).

The rural Thai way of seeing time is not compartmentalised in the same strict way as it is in the industrial world. Eating, sleeping, working and playing tend to get mixed up. The idea of 'a time and place for everything' is very flexibly applied in Thailand.

Days for Doing

There may not be a time and place for everything, but there is (or was, since these habits are dying out today) a day for doing things and a colour for each day. Variations on colour schemes exist; given below are the most common. Thai days, like days in European countries, are named after planets. Thais associate a certain colour with each planet, and it is considered lucky to wear the colour of the day. The fashion conscious ladies of Bangkok in no way stick to this regime, and, although our postman likes the idea, government servants are not given seven different-coloured uniforms to wear on appropriate days.

Superstitions associated with doing certain things on certain days are many; we give only those involved in the dangerous undertaking of having the hair cut. Again, people no longer stick to these beliefs. Few barber shops close on Wednesday!

Day	Colour of dress	Haircut on that day signifies
Sunday	Red	Long life
Monday	Cream (off-white)	Happiness and health
Tuesday	Pink, lilac	Power

Wednesday	Green	Great misfortune
Thursday	Orange	Protection of the angels
Friday	Blue	Lots of luck coming your way
Saturday	Black	Success in important undertakings

Calendars

The Thais recognise that Thai time is not quite the same as *farang* time. This recognition is not limited to questions of punctuality, it also involves different calendars.

The Thais have three calendars, the Gregorian (the same calendar as in the West), the Buddhist Era and the lunar, which is now used only to set the dates of religious ceremonies.

In true Thai fashion, New Year's Day on the Gregorian calendar (introduced in 1899) was celebrated on the first day of *April* until 1941. Thai New Year (the Songkran festival) continues to be celebrated on April 13 each year, although the first month of the lunar year (which Songkran marks the 'beginning' of) is in December!

Just to add to the chronological confusion, the Buddhist Era (B.E.) year in Thailand is one year behind that of Burma, Sri Lanka and India. The bewildered reader will be relieved to hear that B.E. and Gregorian calendars, the only ones used officially, now both begin on the familiar date of January 1. Books and reports, even those written in or translated into English, often carry the B.E. date. To find out how recent they are, the visitor has only to subtract 543 to find the Gregorian equivalent. This easy to remember formula is important, since even those Thais who speak good English usually have a lot of trouble when it comes to translating years.

MONEY

Thais see themselves as a generous, tolerant and contented people lacking in worldly ambition and unhappy about entering into situations of direct competition. Foreign visitors tend to see them in much the same way, a happy people whose material modesty is more than balanced by spiritual wealth. We agree.

Thais are certainly generous and love to treat their friends (and themselves). This apparently altruistic behaviour is not, however, without some self-interest. It increases an individual's status, builds up his entourage of dependent friends and, if he can be consistently generous, gains him a reputation which may bring positions of trust and access to money. This type of behaviour comes close to what anthropologists term 'sympathetic magic', of which plenty of examples exist among the Thais. During the hottest month of the year, April, when water is most scarce, it is squandered in orgies of water battles during the Songkran festival, which can last for weeks in the rural areas and functions to attract water by throwing it around. Thais often behave in much the same way with money.

Songkran, coming at the end of the dry season, inevitably brings rain, but squandermania, unfortunately, doesn't always lead to wealth. If it did, the Thais would be a very rich people.

VIOLENCE

Violence in any form, physical, verbal or mental, and for whatever reason, is detested by Thais. Whenever possible, a sensible man avoids placing himself in a situation of potential violence and behaves in a way that prevents such situations arising or neutralises them if they cannot be avoided.

Cool Hearts

Conflict-avoidance is conceptualised in Thai as *jai yen*, literally 'cool heart', the opposite of *jai rohn*, 'hot heart', overt acts of anger, displeasure and impatience. Whatever the situation, *jai yen* reaction is good and *jai rohn* is bad. The man who meets a difficult situation in a *jai yen* way is admired. If you lose your cool, you lose respect.

So strong is the social pressure to avoid conflict that obvious injustice or abuse may be tolerated with an outwardly submissive

111

attitude. If you listen carefully, you might hear the *tuk-tuk* driver, pulled over to the side of the road by a policeman who seems to be determined to ignore all rules of acceptable social conduct, muttering half to himself and half to the unreasonable force confronting him, '*jai yen nah, jai yen-yen*'.

Superficiality

At their best, *krengjai* attitudes and *jai yen* reactions produce a harmonious society. This can be very attractive to the non-Thai visitor who confines his world to the safety of first-class hotels and the sanity of royal temples. The longer-term visitor will come to understand that this harmony is superficial.

Superficiality or, to put it another way, surface actions of a relationship, are not seen in exactly the same way by a Thai and a westerner. In the west, real 'meaning' is thought to lie some way below the surface. The surface has meaning, but it is not all there is to meaning. No doubt the same is true in Thailand. The difference is that the Thai would tend to accept superficial reality without looking for a deeper meaning. In a sense, *the surface is the meaning* and surface harmony, whatever the motives or feelings of the individuals involved, is real harmony.

Surface Harmony

There are very sound reasons for preserving surface harmony and avoiding conflict rather than trying to resolve it. Firstly, most Thais live in villages, in daily close contact involving periodic cooperation. Secondly, Buddhist dogma makes a virtue of the 'middle path' (avoiding extremes) and detachment; love and hate are recognised as two sides of a single coin and should be treated carefully. A third reason is provided by the spirit beliefs that coexist with Thai Buddhism; anger offends the household spirits and brings bad luck. Fourthly, in a village community, social pressures to conform to norms of conflict-avoidance largely take the place of written law and punishment. (Anybody interested in following up these four points could start with Klausner's book, *Conflict and Communication*, and stop with Mulder's *Everyday Life in Thailand*.)

The last of these four reasons requires some explanation because it can be argued that social pressure is, if not a form of violence, a qualification of the assertion that Thais are tolerant of individual idiosyncrasies. In fact, this tolerance is real enough, but the well-being of the community takes precedence over individual liberty. This situation has been summed up by King Bhumibol as 'individual liberty is restricted by the liberty of others'.

Anger and Conflict

Any individual who openly demonstrates anger threatens the community. The Thai explanation for this process of cause and effect involves reference to the spirit world. Human anger attracts the anger of the spirits. These spirits behave in much the same way as a drunk suffering from *jai rohn* who flings a hand-grenade into a crowd of innocent people in order to get the one person he wants to kill; the spirits heap their displeasure on the whole community in the form of floods, droughts, famines, epidemics or attacks by bandits.

The Thai world view sees violence and tragedy, whether natural or man-made, as the effect of human anger. In an agricultural community this way of seeing things is perfectly logical. Anger disrupts a community and reduces cooperation in important activities such as construction of irrigation systems which can control floods, bring relief from drought and reduce the possibility of famine, low nutrition and epidemics. Anger within a community also reduces its ability to defend itself against bandits. Social norms of conflict-avoidance, supported by an ideology of spirit propitiation, serve very real functions.

The urban situation releases individuals from many of the restraints of public opinion and modern explanations and solutions for disasters undermine belief in the power of the spirit world. Yet, although anger and violence are today part of daily life in any big city, *jai yen* behaviour and the belief in spirits are also very evident, even in the anarchy of Bangkok. The consensus of village community is lacking, but the man who keeps his cool still earns the respect of his friends and workmates.

Self-control

Jai yen keeps Bangkok from blowing apart. The calm faces on a bus packed and overflowing, the crowd sheltering for an hour waiting for the rain to stop, schoolgirls standing in a line in the thin shadow of a lamppost, the only shelter from a blazing sun. *Jai yen* is people in control of themselves, a passive refusal to be ground down, a deep-seated individualism and existentialism; human dignity.

Jai yen has been likened to the French sang-froid. Sang-froid is, however, an exceptional reaction in a nation known for (and perhaps rather proud of) its excitable citizens who often see open, public conflict as a virtue. The French musketeer could fight a duel, kill his enemy and retain his sang-froid. For a Thai, violence is *jai rohn*, he cannot fight and keep his cool.

We see *jai yen* more in terms of the English reserve, a studied non-involvement, a conscious avoidance of the unpleasant or potentially unpleasant. Both are self-imposed constraints on spontaneous behaviour and both are likely, at times, to break down. Perhaps the major difference between the two is that English reserve breaks down into friendship, while Thai *jai yen*, perfectly compatible with friendship, breaks down into violence.

Hot Hearts

When the mask breaks and hearts leap to boiling point, violence ensues. Unfortunately, it is quite impossible to predict at what point this will occur; each heart has an individual thermostat. Some indication is usually given of impending violence, although this may not be immediately evident to the non-Thai. Polite speech becomes less polite until the point of no return is reached when the pronoun for animals and objects, *ke*, is used for 'you'. Alternatively, if somebody is feeling very *jai rohn* but has the sense to remain *krengklua* (afraid), he may try to release his violence on any handy inanimate or animate object, slamming a door, 'accidentally' knocking a glass from the table, ripping the seat of a parked motorcycle, yelling at a child or kicking a dog.

Open violence is today all too frequent. Newspapers are full of reports of attacks by wives against husbands and workers against bosses. Many of these are a result of the sudden snapping of internal controls after a long period of brooding of which the victim might be completely unaware. In recent years there seems to have been a vast increase in the number of sexual organs chopped from sleeping husbands by brooding wives. Even more frequent, and something of more direct concern to the average visitor, is the habit of hiring a professional bully-boy who will poison a dog for a few baht, maim a person to order for a few hundred or kill for a few thousand. Knowing and appreciating the limits of *jai yen* is important for any visitor who wants to live, and perhaps work, for some time in Thailand. The abuse of cool hearts will surely, somehow, bring the wrath of the spirit world down on your head.

SPIRITS

The Thai attitude to spirits is very similar to the Thai attitude to human beings. Some spirits can be trusted and respected; others cannot be trusted and must be feared.

In the Home

Trusted spirits can be members of the family. They are known generally as *phii ruan* (spirits of the home). In the north, these spirits are thought of as deceased family members and are often assigned a special place to live in the house, usually a shelf high up on an inside wall. On this shelf fresh flowers and drink are offered to the family

A spirit house.

ancestors. Their duty is to look after the family's welfare and they will be asked for special help during difficult times (sickness, pending law suit, a job interview, etc.).

Spirit Houses

In Central Thailand, the *phii ruan* have no specific place to live in the house and some young people in Bangkok may never have heard of them. In Bangkok and the surrounding ricelands, the *phra phum* (spirit of the land) is more important. This spirit lives in the spirit house constructed in one corner of the compound. The exact place and time for erection of a spirit house is determined by consulting an astrologer. It is usually placed on top of a wooden or concrete post, high enough to show respect but low enough to permit offerings to be made. Spirit houses are also erected by the sides of roads at accident black spots or sites of past massacres. Individuals set them up in fulfilment of vows and over time a collection of spirit houses can grow into a 'spirit town'.

Spirit houses are usually shaped like a miniature temple. They look something like a birdhouse in the west, but no bird would dare occupy them because the *phra phum* will not allow it. A figure, representing the *phra phum*, carved from wood or moulded from clay, is placed against the far wall facing the door. If the *phra phum* grants a wish he might be given elephants or slaves, represented by similar figures. Some modern *phra phum* even sleep on little beds and we know of one who watches television and drives a Mercedes.

Making Vows

The habit of making a vow and keeping it if the wish is fulfilled is extended to various shrines in Bangkok. This explains why a shrine you walk past every day is suddenly covered in flowers—somebody has won a lottery. The nicely carved little elephants that you see on such shrines are given to the spirit so that he can go for a trip to consult the gods in the sky on Thursday. To take one away might cause the spirit to land right on your head and bring you some very bad luck.

Spirit Types

Apart from family type spirits and spirits of the land, other natural spirits which are 'role specific' and respected are the spirits of rice, water, trees and wind. Each of these has specific powers over the environment and can provide help only within specific areas of influence. Thus, the rice spirit is propitiated on planting and harvest-

A phii gaseu on a Bangkok movie poster.

ing in the hope of getting a good crop, but no matter how great the propitiation, the rice spirit can never protect the house. Such spirits enjoy an inviolable division of labour which might be the envy of a British trade union.

Unfortunately, many members of the spirit world are less predictable, more mobile and far more dangerous. These are the ghosts of dead people who failed to be reborn. There are some good ones, but most of them are rather nasty pieces of work who will wait a long time for rebirth. Some are more powerful than others, but hierarchies are not established as they are in the human world.

The absence of hierarchical norms of behaviour accounts for the unpredictability of these spirits. However, like human beings, they do respond to bribery. Generally, the rule is that the more you bribe a spirit, the more he or she uses power to your advantage.

Some of the most common of these roaming spirits are the *phii tai tang klom* (ghosts of women who die in pregnancy). One of these fierce ladies used to haunt the sois of the Sukhumvit area (where expats tend to live!). She became famous as *Nang Nak Prakanong* and caused all kinds of trouble before she was tricked into Wat Mahabutr on Soi On Nut (soi 72), where her power was neutralised and where, hopefully, she will long remain.

No doubt the prevalence of these ghosts indicates a social fact: the number of Thai women who die in labour. Modern medicine is probably responsible for a decrease in sightings of these *phii* in Bangkok. Significantly perhaps, the *phii tai tang klom* are being edged out by the *phii tai hong*, ghosts of those who died violently!

Particularly nasty are the finicky carnivores known as *phii gaseu*. These gourmands can digest nothing but intestines, preferably of pregnant women. As proof of the saying 'we are what we eat', they take the form of disembodied human heads, glowing as they float through the moonlight, trailing long tails of intestines.

Anti-ghosts

Fortunately, no ghost exists without its 'anti-ghost'. The difficulty comes in locating it. The first step is to identify the evil force that has been causing you to lose badly when gambling or has helped the young girl next door resist your natural charms for so long. For appropriate diagnosis of your problem and help in selecting a strong ally in the spirit world, you require the services of a *mor phii* (spirit doctor) or a *khon song* (trance medium).

Full protection and high virility can be a weighty affair, but this man is leaving nothing to chance.

Charms

Spirit doctors, trance mediums and some monks will provide (for a consideration) an appropriate amulet to protect against danger and misfortune or to ensure love, luck and power. These charms come in three categories, *phra khreuang*, *khreuang-rang* and *khreuang-rang pluk-sek*. *Phra khreuang* are Buddha pendants, or likenesses of famous monks. These are worn around the neck, the more the better.

Khreuang-rang are more specific in function, protecting or aiding within a specified area of influence. Most common of these are tiger teeth, pieces of elephant tusk or buffalo horn, boar tusk and adamantine cat's eyes. They are usually hung around the neck or worn as bracelets. Sometimes, charms with a function as specific as the moulded phallus are worn in other places!

Khreuang-rang pluk-sek are secret formulae. These are usually memorised but can be written down on an object and worn. If they are written, old Khmer letters are used. The memorised kind are usually very specific, one to be used when attacked by robbers, one to protect from accidents, one to help when a special favour is needed from somebody in authority, and so on. The trick is to repeat the appropriate formula for the occasion over and over in your mind, silently sapping the power which threatens you, while keeping your cool. If attacked by bandits, however, the formula, yelled at full volume, might just stop them dead in their tracks—although it is wise to flee the scene at the same time.

Some *khreuang-rang pluk-sek* take the form of tattoos on the body. These serve many purposes. A bird pecking at a *Bo* leaf tattooed on a man's cheek ensures he can win a girl's heart. Hanuman, the monkey of the *Ramayana* epic, tattooed along with appropriate spells, endows the bearer with great strength and stamina.

A girl who finds herself inexplicably attracted to a man and unable to resist his advances may suspect that he has caused a drop of magic oil (usually fat melted from the chin of a woman who died in labour!)

to touch her skin. If she wants to retain her virtue, there is only one sure remedy—a magic tattoo on the forearm.

Whether measures such as these really work and whether the spirit world really exists are, of course, totally irrelevant to belief. Belief in an animated spirit world and the belief that an appropriate charm, spell, or bribe exists to enlist the power of the spirit world in the manipulation of daily life are very important parts of Thai psychological make-up and relate directly to everyday behaviour.

How to Deal with the Spirits

The best way to deal with unfamiliar ghosts and spirits is exactly the same as the way of dealing with living strangers. Firstly, avoid attracting attention to yourself by boasting or doing anything that makes you stand out from the crowd. Secondly, if an unknown power is directed at you, promise it anything in order to get out of an unpleasant situation, and once out of it, employ any means to neutralise that power.

If, in spite of your modest behaviour, you find that you have a spirit on your tail, be prepared to try a double bluff. Make yourself really stand out by doing things in reverse. Have a bath with your clothes on, then take them off. Walk around backwards. Go to bed at dawn and get up at night. This should be enough to totally confuse the spirits (and everybody else!).

These deliberate 'rites of reversal' are, perhaps fortunately, very rarely necessary. Sometimes, however, we do them subconsciously. If you find yourself putting your left leg in your right trouser or putting your shirt on backwards, or your knickers on inside out, watch out, your pre-industrial psyche may have sensed something nasty lurking in the shadows. We hasten to add that the girls in banks and offices wearing cardigans back to front are trying to protect themselves from the air-conditioner, not from wayward spirits!

Such odd behaviour as wearing your clothes inside out is recommended only as a last resort. The best way to stay safe from the spirit world, as every Thai child knows, is to stay calm and stay out of trouble.

Spirits love trouble. Any break in the façade of superficial harmony between living beings brings with it the risk of stirring up unknown and potentially dangerous powers. The best technique for keeping evil at bay is non-involvement. Smile, show respect, but don't show your feelings. If you hate somebody, cast a spell on him, but keep your cool. If you can't keep your heart cool, then flee the scene.

— Chapter Five —

THAIS MEAN BUSINESS

In the 1970s and 1980s Peace Corps volunteers received several months intensive language training and cultural orientation before arrival and more once they arrived in Thailand, before then going off, probably to teach English in a Thai school. Very good. As we turn into the 21st century expat managers, perhaps responsible for a budget of millions of dollars, are expected to pick things up as they go along.

Business and Culture

Thailand, like several other East and Southeast Asian countries, has developed very rapidly in recent years, attracting substantial foreign enterprise and investment. Just about all foreign companies setting up in Bangkok feel the need to appoint at least one expatriate 'manager'.

Unfortunately, they often fail to equip the manager with the linguistic and cultural knowledge which would help him do his job in a strange country. Many Japanese companies now provide cultural orientation and Thai language training to all staff coming to Thailand. They are the exceptions. And they are doing well.

International companies and organisations, used to rotating expatriate management staff between countries, rarely furnish much in the way of orientation. Most embassies consider it enough to have one or two of their nationals conversant with Thai, Thailand and the Thais, the rest of their expat staff is provided with a cultural bubble within which their social and material needs are met more or less as they are back home.

Almost all embassies have national clubs and organisations which are overwhelmingly expat and usually open to anybody living in the country: they might include classes in English, French or German culture and language for Thais. They are unlikely to provide any class in Thai culture and language for their expat nationals. Fine, if the expat is here to attend expat social functions and play with fellow expats. Not quite so fine if he is intent on educating Thais in the ways of his country. Not fine also even if his business is wholly orientated towards the expat community. Not at all fine if the expat is here to manage Thais at work, to reach annual objectives, and to make money.

Thais mean business. Not all of them are willing or able to cope with a range of expat cultures, attitudes and languages in order to do business with foreigners. If foreigners want the business, they will have to be prepared for the fact that norms of business management are not always the same in Thailand and in the west.

The Expat Manager

Forget any ideas about 'one-minute management' and be prepared to spend time with your staff, mostly on an individual basis when directly related to work tasks, and on a group basis for social occasions. There is a place for the weekly staff meeting which will serve for you to provide information received from headquarters and summarise local events of the week, with praise when due but not criticism. Such meetings should not be seen as a short cut to delegating work for the week ahead or appraising in any but the broadest sense the week gone past. A few questions might be raised, but don't expect much in the way of 'brainstorming'.

In addition to managing your staff, you will, to a varying degree depending on the nature of your business, need to be in touch with Thai business contacts, government officials, and influential people. You will need to build alliances and know your enemies and how to neutralise them. You will need an information system which amounts to a genteel spy network. In all of this, you will certainly need some capable and well placed assistance.

The Compradore

All of the successful earlier foreign business enterprises in Thailand survived because they worked through a Thai compradore, a person of influence who owed his loyalty to Thailand but who received money from foreigners. A compradore held an important and respected position.

The term 'compradore' is still in use in English and in Thai. In English it now has pejorative connotations related to the spread of European imperialism. In Thai it has lost its original meaning and usually now refers to a financial broker (without any pejorative undercurrents). Although use of the term had best be avoided lest HQ calls back its nut-case representative, the foreign entrepreneur or manager will certainly need a modern compradore of some sort if he is to survive and prosper. Call him or her what you will—partner, deputy, assistant, consultant, or even secretary—but know that an efficient compradore is necessary to operations.

The role, power and recompense of the compradore will vary according to the reasons he is employed. However, even those foreigners who have established successful small enterprises in the Kingdom entirely through their own efforts need a Thai partner. A foreigner might have lived in the country most of his life, speak totally fluent Thai, and be accepted by Thais as Thai. He could even have a national reputation and access to the highest of social circles. He thinks Thai. And because of this, he plays it safe. Let others, preferably Thais, praise him if they will; he will humbly and publicly attribute everything he has achieved to his Thai mentor.

For most expat managers in Thailand, there is no question of fame and real fortune. They are interested in the shortest route to efficient and profitable management. Your compradore will tell you the way. Day-to-day bureaucratic problems, which can stifle your company and you, will disappear. When you come to the table to sign contracts, it will be for symbolic discussion, probably some last-minute light-hearted ritual of bargaining and commemorative photographs: all the work has been done behind the scenes but not behind your back by your compradore and the person in the other camp with whom he or she went to school. Problems of project implementation, import and export regulations, building permits and so on: your compradore is there to smooth things over.

Your modern version compradore will owe loyalty to you as well as the company. Most likely he or she has really been running the Thailand part of the empire for years already and you have only to fit in and make yourself liked. If such arrangements already exist, count your blessings. Disrupt them at your peril.

If you find yourself replacing a failed manager, there may be nobody performing the compradore's role. Look carefully around your staff. They were probably recruited because of high education and proficiency in English, qualities which are becoming increasingly available but are still very much valued. Just a few years ago a really well educated Thai was rare enough that he or she was likely to know personally many of the like-educated (and well placed) and to be related to at least some. Pay particular attention to the middle-aged.

Decide as quickly as you can if you simply need someone who knows his way around customs procedures or if you are flying much higher. A compradore with court connections is not a must if you are managing a restaurant on Patpong: an ex-policeman could be helpful.

If there is no one available to fill the role, you will have to recruit. Be careful: employ a Thai *only* because of good social contacts and he could turn out to be inefficient, dishonest and hard to get rid of. The surest way to get the reasonably sure assistance of a good compradore is to poach one from another foreign company, which is not easy and will certainly involve offering much more money and non-taxable incentives.

Reorganising

However good your compradore, he or she will not manage your staff and is not likely to be doing much in the way of routine office work. Hopefully, routine administrative work will be carried out efficiently with a minimum of checking. If it is not, very discreetly switch functions around a bit among your staff until you are satisfied. Take your time, but not too long. It is expected that a new boss might have some changes to make.

The good manager will make it look, at least on the surface, as if everybody involved in the changes is getting increased responsibilities that will place them in line for promotion. Let your staff come to understand, without telling them, that within the limitations set by company budgets, rules and regulations (and up to you to decide how far these can be bent—in the company's interest of course) you will follow traditional Thai patronage practice and reward those who follow and obey. Showing maximum concern for those who work well and support you does not, of course, mean you ignore production. It will be fully understood that those who do not follow and obey will be exterminated.

Having satisfied yourself that your organisational structure is sound, you can sit back a bit and appear to relax. You have time now to get to know your staff a bit, not too much, be friendly but not friends, and to make the workplace more pleasant and yourself more popular. Time to enjoy it all and at the same time really get down to work. Of course, as you would have guessed by now, getting down to work doesn't mean quite the same thing for the western manager and his Thai staff ...

WORK

The Thai word *ngan* means both 'work' and 'party'. It does not follow from this that Thais cannot distinguish between work and party and it certainly should not be assumed that Thais would just as soon go to work as they would go to a party. Rather, it implies that whenever it is possible to turn work into a party, Thais will do so.

The industrial mind, more used to thinking of work and party as opposites, may find this single Thai concept somewhat inscrutable at first. The origin of the term fully explains the mystery.

In the agricultural setting, where most Thais live and work, people come together in groups linked by kinship and friendship to do difficult jobs or work requiring a larger workforce than one family can provide. Thus, *tham ngan* (to work) means literally 'make (up a) party'.

Cooperation

In the modern urban setting, an invitation to *ngan* in a friend's house does not mean that everybody should come armed with a spade and ready to dig the garden, but it still implies an element of collective work. Such work, like most work in Thailand, is done by the women. The men might help out to the extent of rigging a tarpaulin outside so that they can sit in the shade and drink Mekhong whisky while waiting for the women to prepare the food. Work done together is much more fun than the usual daily cooking chores.

Most people would much rather prepare a party than transplant rice seedlings. Such work is never likely to be much fun, but working

'Our backs to the sky, our faces to the ground ... forever.' (Farmers' saying)

together at least makes it bearable. Certain economic benefits are to be gained from cooperative patterns of work organisation, but it is noticeable that the total number of people coming together is usually much greater than the minimum number required to reap these benefits. Nobody wants to be left out. This is not because of any altruistic feeling of helping one's neighbour, since all labour contributed by one family to another is precisely and directly reciprocated in kind. To be left out of the work would mean being left out of the party.

Cooperative 'labour exchange' involves the host's family feeding all of the work-party before and after work; roles are reversed as hosts change from day to day. Thus, at certain times of the year at least, 'work' and 'party' are, if not exactly the same, very much interrelated.

Most Thais live and work in an agricultural setting, where people come together to tham ngan—work, or literally 'make up a party'.

During the working day, backs are bent but there is always the chance to assess the strength and patience of a possible future bride or son-in-law. And when backs stretch up and sit down in a patch of shade for a while, there are friends to chat and eat with.

Motivation

Often people working side by side on transplant or harvest enter into friendly 'competition' to be the first to finish a line. Like bus-drivers

131

racing side by side in Bangkok, such contests add a fun element to what would otherwise be a hard and dreary job and provide short-term incentives to work hard when one man alone might feel an over-whelming desire to sit under a tree and have a smoke.

These traditional patterns of motivation are often lacking in an urban work situation. The Thais will try as best they can to recreate them. Successful offices and factories are usually those where people enjoy their work and have plenty of opportunities to come together for social activity. The expat manager working in Thailand, used perhaps to treating his long-industrialised workers to one office bus-trip to Brighton each year and a barrel of beer at Christmas, might be advised to allow a somewhat greater percentage of running costs to be spent on fun and games.

In Thailand, few workers are happy with purely economic incen-tives if a job is no fun. Fortunately, plenty of occasions exist for organising parties, and the expat manager's role is usually limited to sitting back and enjoying it, perhaps giving a short speech praising the work of everybody and indicating future expansion of the company and, of course, picking up a large part of the bill when the party is over.

Any opening enterprise, or one reopening, relocating or building a new wing or branch office will invite nine monks to bless the new adventure/location; the monks will be fed, then the workers.

The *Kathin* outing in November/December is the nearest the Thais get to the day-trip-to-Brighton. At this time in almost every work-place employing Thais, an organising committee will be formed almost spontaneously. People on this committee will be the natural social leaders of any office or workplace. The department manager might not be on it; the receptionist might.

The *Kathin* committee will arrange hire of a bus, collect money from all employees, buy the new robes and other things to be presented to the monks (this is the purpose of *Kathin*) and make absolutely sure there is plenty to eat and drink for the merit makers. Then everybody goes off on a fun trip. They could simply go to the

Wat next door, but the chances are they will drive across the country and make the donation at a *Wat* few of them have ever seen before. These trips and similar activities serve to make a place of work a place of fun. When work stops being fun, it rapidly slows down and sometimes stops completely. The Thais do not have an international reputation for discipline and staying power. New activities may be enthusiastically taken up only to be dropped when rewards are not immediately forthcoming or when work becomes too boring. In the agricultural setting, social pressures from family and neighbours might be enough to keep an individual at the job until the next party comes along. Such pressures cannot exist to the same extent in offices and factories.

Family

Most large-scale urban work situations involve bringing people who have no common links of kinship or neighbourhood into daily interaction. Even so, a surprising number of established institutions in Bangkok are staffed largely on a family basis. If the newcomer goes to learn Thai at the AUA, he will find that just about all the Thai teachers seem to be related. In that situation, something of a family enterprise has been recreated and has been working extremely well for a long, long time. Teachers help each other out and are obviously enjoying what would otherwise be a very dull job indeed (repeating the same lessons over and over every five weeks for years on end). Both teachers and students benefit from the pleasant relationships existing between staff members.

Apart from the universal small family business and some note-worthy exceptions, relationships engendered in the family village setting have no obvious application to most urban patterns of work organisation. However, they remain important to an individual's chances of finding work. A villager from the northeast could arrive in Bangkok one day and, if his uncle is a taxi driver, be driving a taxi the next (even if he has to ask his passengers the way!).

Family relations can help 'productivity', as in the case of the AUA, and they can help individuals (but not necessarily taxi passengers); they can also create some problems.

Nepotism

Nepotism can influence job appointments and selection of contract tenders. The non-Thai executive will not be under social pressure to help his relatives (unless he marries a Thai) but he should be aware that the Thai he asks for advice may be socially obliged to place personal relationships before questions of productivity.

Nepotism is not necessarily negative. It could be seen as an attempt to recreate something of the rural ideal, where economic and social relationships are not separated as they are in an urban environment.

Modernisation and urbanisation have tended, in a very short time, to reverse the ancient and natural social order of the Thais. To a Thai, a life spent more in the company of complete strangers than together with trusted family members is an unnatural and insecure life.

A sales manager who passes over better qualified and more experienced applicants in order to give the vacant assistant sales manager's job to his nephew, may get a very good assistant he can trust. However, if he knows full well that his nephew is lazy, unintelligent and would do the job badly, he is still likely to feel some obligation to support his application, although with somewhat less enthusiasm.

In our view, nepotism (favouring family members over strangers) is a very natural thing in any country with a strong agricultural tradition. While managers must obviously be aware of its possible negative effects, too strong an attempt to stamp it out might seriously disturb the workplace and retard the development of a 'working community'.

Job Accumulation

While nepotism may be natural and, under certain conditions, might lend stability and continuity to a labour force, it is difficult to see any advantages to that other prevalent urban work habit, job accumulation. The sleepy-eyed government clerk may be selling real-estate at night. The fact that your executive secretary stays late in the office after you have gone home may have nothing to do with her official workload but a lot to do with the private typing and telephoning she does on the side to help her husband's export business. The public relations officer who disappears for two hours every Thursday might be giving English lessons to the Thai boss of the office next door.

The reason so many people are working so long, if not so hard, is a very simple one: money, or the lack of it. Thailand is at a point in its development-a-go-go where cars, condominiums and other goodies churned out at a furious pace during the big boom remain tantalisingly in reach for many, but only if some protracted stretching takes place.

Even the rich go in for job collecting. The motive for doing so is, however, likely to be status rather than, or as well as, money. In 1973, shortly before he was overthrown from power, Field Marshal Prapass gave a speech entitled 'One Job is Enough'. In this speech he urged people to give up the habit of job accumulation and concentrate on doing one job well. In a press report of this speech, the Field Marshal was referred to as Field Marshal Prapass, Deputy Prime Minister, Interior Minister, Acting Director-General of the Police Department, Deputy Supreme Commander of the Armed Forces, Commander-in-Chief of the Royal Thai Army, Chairman of the Board of Directors of the Bangkok Bank, and Chairman of the Hill Tribes Development Committee in the Communist Suppression Operation Command.

CRITICISM

In Thailand, face-to-face criticism is seen as a form of violence. It hurts people and threatens superficial harmony. Disturbance of the peace is, for the Thai, a totally negative concept. Open criticism is therefore rarely, if ever, entered into with any positive intention of improving a conflict situation. The act of criticism is at best a sign of bad manners, at worst a deliberate attempt to offend.

'Constructive' Criticism

In the west, it is thought (or pretended) to be possible and even admirable for two people to disagree in public, be critical of each other's ideas in a meeting, agree to disagree or to reach a constructive compromise, remain friends and go off for a drink together after work. Maybe some *farang* do manage this extraordinary feat, which smacks of sadism-masochism to the Thai way of seeing. Do not expect Thais to behave in the same way. Thais are unlikely to consider whether a criticism is 'fair' or 'unfair'; friends do not act violently towards each other. If you offend a Thai by criticising him in public, he might avoid you forever more.

In Thailand, forget all you have come to believe about constructive criticism. Almost all criticism is destructive. Clearly, Thai and *farang* do not see criticism in the same way. The difference is an essential part of the great divide between conflict-resolution and conflict-avoidance. In the west, differences of opinion may be intentionally aired in public. This is considered a healthy state of affairs. If critical opposition is lacking, one person may deliberately take the role of 'devil's advocate', setting out the 'other side of the coin' in the interests of 'fair play'. A synthesis of opposing views or a choice between two or more alternatives would ideally be made when all facts and viewpoints had been clearly stated.

In Thailand, differences of opinion exist but critical expression of these differences is carefully avoided. Resolution, if any, of conflicting points of view is less a matter of dialectical debate than of behind-the-scenes manipulation.

Criticism is not only disliked, it is also regarded as destructive to the social system. The superior is supposed to decide, the inferior is supposed to obey. To criticise a superior is to question the idea that the superior is always right. To criticise an inferior would suggest either that the inferior is responsible for making decisions or that the orders given him by the superior were inadequate or that the superior had made a mistake in entrusting the job to somebody who was incompetent to do it. Criticising an inferior in public would also impress on all present the superior's bad manners as much as the inferior's inefficiency.

If a superior is criticised, he would most likely respond by removing the source of criticism. Even if the inferior's comments make sense and could save a lot of money or a lot of lives, they are unlikely to be considered. In the unlikely event that such criticism is acted upon, the inferior is likely to gain nothing and is most likely to be sacked, demoted or transferred.

The inferior criticised by a superior cannot remove the source of the discomfort but he can remove himself. As fast as possible, flee the scene. If he does not, he has to accept public shame. Such public acceptance is inevitably accompanied by private resentment. A Thai can brood for months. During this time, orders received from the superior-critic may be slowly executed, deliberately delayed or delegated to people not equipped to do the job, perhaps with a comment like, 'the boss told me to give you this to do'.

The taboo against open criticism to an individual's face does not extend to covert criticism behind the back and a prolonged gossip campaign could reduce a superior's popularity and harm productivity. Such passive resistance is very difficult to counter. Certainly, it cannot be removed by further doses of criticism.

Indirect Criticism

What then is the poor *farang* boss to do in Thailand? Must he put up with lateness and poor quality work and make no complaints that could possibly be construed as criticism of individuals?

Maybe. Putting up with it might be more profitable than trying to put it down. At least, recognise that you are in a very different work situation. The boss respected by the workers as 'hard but fair' back in Germany is not likely to accomplish great things in Thailand unless he wears a muzzle. The successful *farang* boss in Thailand is often the one who is very popular with the workers and interferes with them as little as possible. Certainly he does not roll up his sleeves and show them how to do their job. Instead he might take a lesson from the white elephant and criticise by praising while punishing through kindness.

White Elephants

White elephants are given to the King as a mark of respect. Symbols of national peace and prosperity, they are well looked after according to a set and expensive procedure.

In the past, a King would honour his nobles by giving them white elephants to look after. The expense involved in maintenance would pose no problems for those who held favour in the court since a gift of land would also be made. It has been suggested, however, that white elephants were a double-edged sword. They could increase a noble's status or they could drain the purse of the lesser noble, perhaps one trying to climb a bit too fast above his station.

A noble who had gained the court's displeasure need not be criticised. He would simply be sent a white elephant (without a gift of land). The 'honour' could not be refused. The elephant would do no work and could not be sold or given away. The offending noble would take care to avoid receiving any similar honours in the future by adjusting his behaviour or ambitions.

White elephants are not recommended as gifts to subtly put the maid back in her place or to reduce the secretary's trips to the canteen, but the principle of indirect criticism is appropriate.

Open or public criticism by Thais, of the kind one politician will make of another to the media, is tantamount to an act of war— hopefully of the cold rather than the hot type. It takes place all the time between individuals belonging to rival groups. It does not take place publicly between members of a single group. Neither does it take place within a group—unless the group is splitting up or an individual has decided to attach himself to a patron in a contending faction.

Ticking Off Gently

Being indirect does not mean being sarcastic. Thais have a great sense of humour but they don't like sarcasm. 'Did your bus get cut in half by a train again this morning?' is not an example of indirect criticism and it is likely to make a worker later the next morning, not earlier.

In the west, an employee late for work is ticked off immediately on arrival. The crime is fresh, the punishment given and hopefully all can then get down to work.

In Thailand, the employee could wait until after lunch or even the next day, then receive some praise for good work (nothing too patronising—'that's nicely typed' is quite enough to make her like and respect you). This praise would be followed up by a few questions of a personal nature which might bring the reply 'mind your own bloody business' back in Islington but which, in Thailand, would be regarded as a superior showing interest in the welfare of his subordinates. Is everything all right at home? Has the baby recovered? Are you still living at the same place? That's a long way, isn't it? And, if you really need to drive the message home, nothing stronger or more sarcastic than—how long does it take you to get to work?

That should be enough. If it is not and the offender keeps right on offending, decide whether the deviant behaviour is really upsetting the work schedules. If it is not and you are simply enforcing rules in order to maintain overall discipline, you might be better off back in Germany. If there is some real reason to make somebody turn up at 7.30 instead of 7.50, make a point of 'seeing' the person involved alone. Be indirect, even at this stage. If you are told a list of personal problems which seem to have no bearing on the offending behaviour pattern and which you suspect are complete fabrications, listen sympathetically since this is a mark of a correct superior/inferior relationship (the superior does *not* tell his problems in return).

At some point in this quiet chat you do have to mention clearly the subject involved. A *farang* boss, trying to be reasonable, might think the best way is to explain the importance of keeping the rules—you have to be here at 7.30 otherwise Nit and Noy cannot get in and Lek and Toy might miss the mailman. A better way might be to fall back on the 'leader principle' and bring the whole weight of the Thai system to your aid. Everybody has a superior; make full use of yours.

Passing the Buck

Make it clear that your superiors hold you responsible for your workers' behaviour. If your secretary doesn't turn up on time, you not her are going to get into trouble. Nit and Noy and Lek and Toy are not as important to her as her boyfriend who keeps her up late at night, but everything and everybody is less important than the system.

If you want to express dissatisfaction with a maid's services, the same process of 'setting out the system' can be used. The *farang* wife tells the maid that the master is unhappy with the *wife*, who should be running the house. If you are single you are unlikely to have any problems, but you should, of course, get married as soon as possible before your entire life is taken over by your maid. Marrying the maid is not the answer; many *farang* have tried and all find they gain a wife but lose a maid.

For this technique of passing-the-buck-to-the-superior-once-removed to work properly, the superior making the complaint must be *liked* by the person being indirectly criticised. So following through with some praise for things done right is a good move. If you can't find anything to praise, a bag of expensive cream cakes will make most people like you.

How to Criticise

Indirect criticism is a subtle art and the same format cannot be followed time after time. But the following basic ground rules should act as some kind of guide.

1. Avoid public confrontation at all costs.
2. See the person yourself.
3. Pick the best time for the talk, preferably when things are going well, never when you are angry.
4. Balance any criticism with praise using a ratio of ten parts praise to one part criticism.
5. Be indirect and diplomatic, offering criticisms as suggestions if possible.
6. Be nice all the time and buy lots of cream cakes for everybody.

The most important of these rules is the last one. Being nice instead of asserting your authority nearly always pays.

Complaints

When you buy a new clock and it falls apart after two days. When the plumber repairs the leak by tying one of your handkerchiefs around the water pipe. When the car comes back from repair with an extra 1000 km on the clock. Complaints are in order.

In circumstances like these it is not easy to be polite, friendly and private. But if people like you, they will do things for you or knock something off your bill or do it right next time. There are, of course, limits to being nice. Thailand may teach you yours.

Questions

The Thai reluctance to criticise is extended to asking questions, if these could in any way imply a criticism. Since any question asked in a lecture hall or seminar room would suggest either that the lecture or speech was less than perfect or that the questioner was incapable of understanding, very few questions ever get asked. University lecturers can ask after every lecture 'Any questions?' and never get one. Some may get a few questions a couple of days or a couple of months after the lecture is over. Such questions are always asked in private and always wrapped up in a way that demonstrates quite clearly that the wretched student is too dim to understand the clear and brilliant lecture given.

Although *farang* lecturers and teachers love to bemoan the 'lack of intellectual stimulation' and complain among themselves of the rote-learning education system which discourages critical evaluation

The high status of all teachers is given ceremonial expression on one day of the year, when all students and schoolchildren honour their teachers with beautifully made gifts of flowers.

and punishes originality, they all enjoy working in Thailand. Most of them enjoy it precisely because the students are so uncritical and well-mannered.

If these teachers are good at their job, they allow time and make opportunities for students to consult them in private and incorporate any points raised in such talks in the next lecture without making any direct reference to the questioner. Working within the system in this way takes no more time than the lecturer spends back home trying to be smarter than everybody else in the lecture hall. It is certainly a lot easier on the nerves and, when the answer to a question is not known, a lot safer.

Other foreigners who come to work in Thailand generally get much better pay than lecturers and teachers, but enjoy a much lower status (although probably a higher one than they had back home).

Teachers at tertiary level in Thailand are referred to as *ajarn*, an honorific title that can also be used for monks. The term *ajarn* simply oozes with respect and status, although a bit less so than it did a few years ago. The businessman's title of *nai hang* does imply respect, but it has nothing like the same status. The businessman has mere money to compensate him for the fact that meetings, conferences and seminars involving Thais are always dull affairs.

Anything interesting and important seems to get said over tea before or after the ritual coming together of 'the seminar'. Any damp fireworks are inevitably thrown by a couple of *farang* while Thai participation is usually limited to an occasional yawn.

Conforming to the Taboo

For a *farang* working in Thailand, understanding Thai sensitivities and the criticism taboo is one thing, conforming to it (or, as some say, 'pandering' to it) is quite another. Some would argue that the *farang* should not change his behaviour since he was recruited precisely because of his ability to analyse critically and to act on his analysis in a way that a Thai would find difficult to do.

143

Some *farang* go so far as to suggest that western professional standards contain an ethic which requires open criticism. The line would go that the needs of patients in a hospital and students in a university must come before personal sensitivities of the staff. What is a *farang* doctor to do if he sees a senior Thai doctor prescribing a lethal dose of arsenic? What is a *farang* lecturer to do if he discovers a university professor delegating the marking of examination papers to his maid?

Perhaps the first thing you should do if you find yourself in either of these unlikely situations is to decide exactly what your motive is in making an intervention. Is it to belittle the doctor or professor and prove yourself superior (an acceptable game in the *farang* world but not in the Thai) or is it to help the patients and students in question? If you have the first motive, any boost to your ego will be temporary and the longer-term effects on your career in Thailand could be disastrous. Whether you intend to help yourself or to help the students or patients in question, open criticism may not be the best way of doing things.

Quiet Intervention

Even in these extreme circumstances, the Thai in your position is likely to look for a way to remedy the situation while avoiding confrontation.

The doctor is most unlikely to leave the victims to their fate with, 'well, must be their *karma*, guess they had it coming to them.' He would try to intervene quietly. Perhaps he would simply change the prescription from arsenic to aspirin after the senior doctor had left the room and ask him later how long it has been since he had a holiday. Or, in the examination case, a Thai lecturer might offer the professor, who of course has a thousand demands on his genius, the lecturer's own services in helping the professor mark the papers: 'I hesitate to offer, but I am sure I would learn a great deal if you would allow me to work through those scripts.' Situation corrected and career enhanced. A million times safer and more effective than sending a pile of your own unmarked scripts to the professor's maid.

If such subtle intervention is impossible, other tactics are required. As the senior doctor measures out the arsenic while insisting that the patient drinks it all immediately, the junior doctor, before the lunge to save the patient's life, might try the self-ignorance ploy which would allow his senior to change his mind without losing face. 'Excuse me, sir. What is that the patient is taking? Did you say ascorbic acid, sir? What sort of effect does ascorbic acid have in cases like this, sir?' With any luck the senior might reply 'Ascorbic acid? No, I didn't say that. That would have no effect at all. I said aspirin, but I seem to have got hold of the wrong bottle. Nurse, where is the aspirin?' Such subtlety saves lives, makes friends out of enemies and helps your career by making you look a fool. 'Arsenic? Wouldn't rat poison be better?' is not the thing to say.

GRAFT

Few Thais favour bribery and corruption but few would refuse a present offered for a small service rendered. Western businessmen are reluctant to admit participation in such activities, but most are aware that if they want to be sure goods get to the port in one piece, are cleared in time and are loaded onto the right ship, they must have somebody, somewhere, looking after their interests with an incentive greater than that inspired by the basic wage.

The Thais say, "Look after an elephant and eat its poo-poo." This loses a little in translation but basically means that if you care well for something valuable, certain valuable droppings will (legitimately) come your way.

Bribery

Gunnar Myrdal suggests in *Asian Drama* that among multinational companies in Asia, the Japanese are the most willing to pay bribes to secure trading and manufacturing advantages over their competitors and to ensure smooth day-to-day running of their organisations. They are closely followed by the West Germans, French and Americans.

Large-scale bribery usually involves 'go-betweens'. In this role, the compradores serve much the same functions as marriage go-betweens did in the early stages of marriage negotiations in the past, to prevent embarrassment to either party.

Opening the Mouth

We have already emphasised that a good go-between can be invaluable to the foreign businessman who would otherwise waste much time and money locating the key man in a government department or in a rival agency. The efficient compradore will let you know in confidence when somebody requires 'money to open the mouth' (to speak in favour of, and actively pursue, your interests).

In the absence of a professional middleman, who looks after the company's interests generally and might be given a highly-paid 'consultant' position, specific-purpose middlemen arise from time to time. A clerk in a government office might turn up on behalf of his superior and inform the foreigner that a specific sum of money is required before a service can be performed. There is, of course, no way of knowing if the junior is telling the truth and this is why the major portion of the bribe is only paid upon successful completion of the service. A middleman is a speculator. If he fails to achieve the results, he gets nothing.

Money doesn't always go to the top man of an organisation. A junior member drawing up bids for a contract can provide one bidder with valuable information on the competition and present one bid in a more favourable way than others. When the bids get to the committee stage, one member 'opening his mouth' might be enough. No point in bribing all committee members if you can bribe one man who has the chairman's ear. Having the chairman's ear is most likely to mean that the largest cut will find its way to the chairman. A junior who acted on his own initiative and pocketed the cash would lose job and career if discovered.

Expat companies and organisations not only take part in bribery, they are victims of it. The foreign manager should be aware that a sub-contract does not always go to the most efficient company. Attempting to limit the consequences of this possibility, some companies prefer to split work into two or more contracts, intending to maintain a certain competition for a period before making a firm decision in favour of one party. This can be a dangerous course of action. The companies involved will certainly enter into competition but this might not be limited to demonstration of comparative efficiencies and everybody involved might spend more time trying to knock out the competition than in actively doing the job.

Alternatively, they might cooperate and agree to up the price while sharing the benefits. This is particularly likely when the two competing companies just happen to have the same directors, a coincidence which seems to happen a lot in Thailand.

Invisibility

Bribery is as invisible as the spirit world. Certainly it exists, but it does not appear in the end-of-year accounts. It is therefore very difficult to guess whether the incidence of bribery is higher in Thailand than elsewhere. Even if everybody knows exactly where the money for Boonpop's holiday in Phuket came from, nobody talks about it.

The act of taking bribes is referred to in Thai as 'eating'. Everybody has to eat.

Chapter Six

THE LIFE CIRCLE

CEREMONY

Ceremony, like power, is amoral. It is yet another way of manipulating known and unknown forces. Secret societies, boy scouts, gangsters, spirit mediums, policemen, little old ladies and newborn babies; in Thailand every organisation and every individual takes part in ceremony. Birth and rebirth cause suffering. The many ceremonies of Thailand are part of man's attempt to overcome that suffering and break the circle.

Private and Public

If you come home to find your colour T.V. set missing and burning incense and flowers in its place, it is because the *khamoy* took the time

Even the most dignified of ceremonies, like the Royal Ploughing Ceremony held each year to mark the start of the agricultural cycle on Sanam Luang field, next to the Grand Palace in Bangkok, is good fun.

to placate the spirits of the house and ensure his safe getaway before fleeing the scene. He might never have got into the house at all had you gone to the trouble of keeping the spirits happy, or maybe the real blame lies with the person who built the house, who perhaps skimped on the house-warming ceremony.

Apart from the private *khamoy* escape ceremony, which is dying out as *khamoys* lose their panache, most others take place in public either on the street or in the *Wat*, or both, and show no sign at all of dying out for at least one very good reason: they are good fun.

No public ceremony is taboo for the non-Thai and your presence will be welcomed, as long as you follow the basic rules of good manners. Not all of these are as easy and obvious as 'shoes off at temple door'.

At the end of the Royal Ploughing Ceremony, crowds rush onto the field to collect some of the royal grains, which they mix with their seed stock to ensure a good harvest.

Comfortable Fun

Strolling through the grounds of an upcountry *Wat*, you are welcomed by a group of villagers having lunch and, at the inevitable invitation, you sit down and join them. Bottles of rice whisky are passed back and forth. Cigarettes, hand-rolled in leaves, are lit and relit. People are chatting and joking and everything is very *sabay* (comfortable) and *sanuk* (good fun). What's going on? A wedding, a big win on the lottery, somebody's birthday? No, none of these. Chances are it's a funeral.

Unless you are Irish, you might be a little surprised to see people enjoying themselves at a funeral. In Thailand, whenever people get together to eat and drink, it is fun. This in no way demonstrates lack of respect for the dead. Plenty of tears have been shed in private and in public before you came on the scene. Once the body has been cremated, the dead is on his way to a new life. If the deceased was a good person, the next life will be better than the last: reason to rejoice, not to sorrow. And if the deceased wasn't all he might have been, it is only good manners to ignore that at his funeral and, for the sake of his family, behave as if you are sure he would be reborn as a prince and not a puppy.

One Continuous Ceremony

Life in Thailand often seems like one continuous ceremony. There is no end to it. We have place to consider only the major life-cycle ceremonies: birth, puberty, ordination, marriage and death. We pick five out of a multitude not because there are any real do's and taboos (apart from those already mentioned) for the visitor to follow if he should be present at any of these occasions, but because they show us a lot about Thais. Particularly, they demonstrate the compatibility of Buddhist and animistic (belief in spirits) aspects of life in Thailand.

Some characteristics of Thai ceremony are so common that the visitor cannot help but wonder about them. The most obvious of these are a sacred white thread, the number three, auspicious timing, and money.

White Thread

If your wrists are tied up, don't call for the police until you are sure your host is not making a gesture of welcome. Tying pieces of white thread, called *sai sin*, onto the wrists (but not tying the wrists together!) is a way of wishing somebody safety and good health.

The white thread is found in many ceremonies and usually takes the form of a circle. All participants at a pre-ordination ceremony sit in a circle holding a single long thread between the thumb and first finger of both hands, which are raised in a *wai*. At funerals, the thread is carried in a circle three times around the crematorium. At weddings the thread links the heads of the couple being married.

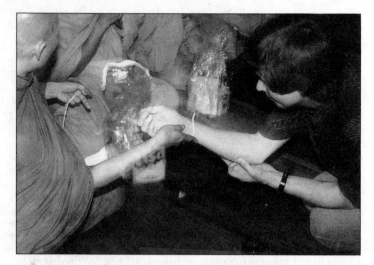

A monk ties sai sin onto a farang's wrist.

The white thread works as a kind of spiritual telegraph, carrying merit along a line or around a circle. When circles of this thread are tied on your wrists, they serve to help you retain all your good power, while protecting you from the potential dangers of the spirit world.

To refuse *sai sin*, if it is offered, is like refusing a man's hospitality. However, although the thread is sacred, or semi-sacred, in Buddhist ceremony, it is only as sacred as good manners when tied around the wrist. One Christian missionary told us he felt as if he were being strangled when *sai sin* were tied on him, but most non-Thais find that the biggest problem with *sai sin* is that they don't know what to do with it once they have got it.

Some visitors find their wrists covered in *sai sin* and, afraid to offend by taking it off, wait forever for it to drop off. One *farang* we know had his wrists tied up just before leaving the northeast, where the custom is particularly rampant, to return home to England. A great lover of the Thais and fearer of spirits, he waited for two threadbare years back in the UK before the circles finally disintegrated and fell off naturally. People looked at him rather strangely in the pub.

It is somewhat rude to take *sai sin* off right in front of the person who has just so charmingly tied it on. But it is quite all right to do so when you have left them and (to play it safe with the spirits) after arriving back home. Ideally, it should be kept on for three days or longer.

Three

Number three, you will notice, occurs time after time and, of course, after time. *Buddha*, *Dharma* (the teachings of the Lord Buddha), *Sangha* (the monastic order). All good things come in lots of three.

Timing

Along with threads and the number three, many ceremonies also have the idea of timing. Everybody, including the King and government leaders, consult astrologers when conducting important ceremonies or implementing important decisions. Important firsts, like putting up a spirit house, laying the first brick or board of a home and sowing the first seed, together with dangerous, chancy things like setting off on an important mission to slay a dragon or getting married, all require trips to the professional astrologer or the local amateur fortune-teller, who will set a propitious time for the event (usually very early in the morning). If your Thai friend invites you to come to his wedding between 6.19 and 6.27 a.m., he means it. This is one occasion when things happen on time.

Money

Money, the fourth common characteristic, speaks for itself. It is often in open evidence in Thai ceremonies. Sometimes it is used symbolically, but more often it is simply an ostentatious display of the host's

Important 'firsts' (openings, sowing of seeds, new arrivals, etc.) require ceremony. Here His Holiness the Supreme Patriarch anoints the nose of the Thai Airways Company's third Boeing 737 before it goes into service.

status and power. Ceremonies vary in grandeur according to the wealth of the people involved, but even the very poor have something of a ceremony at important stages in the life cycle. Money circulates at these events according to well-established norms of reciprocity.

Money usually changes hands inside envelopes. These may be passed to one side unopened, but someone somewhere will note exactly who gave what in order for the family to reciprocate when roles are reversed and hosts become guests.

The non-Thai visitor is, of course, outside this circle. Never mind, you will still be fed. Without thinking of anything as vulgar as paying for your dinner, you might like to pursue a course of 'instant reciprocity' at religious ceremonies, which can be very expensive for the host. This is quite acceptable. Don't count the money out, but the price of a good meal is all right (more if a good friend or colleague is directly involved). With or without an envelope, hand the money directly to your host explaining that you wish to *tham boon* (make merit). He then grants you a favour by accepting your money, rather than you granting him a favour by giving it. This is very much like the feeling of everybody involved in the giving of food to monks on the morning almsround. Far from begging or receiving charity, the monks provide laymen with an opportunity to make merit; it is the laymen who feel gratitude and offer thanks through the *wai*.

One of the most obvious examples of ostentatious use of money is the taking of a 'money-tree' for presentation to the *Wat*. A money-tree is a miniature tree, formed from sprigs of branches, with banknotes stuck on as leaves. It is carried by the family (or leading members of an organisation) through the streets with much dancing and drum playing to make everybody aware of what is going on. If you are held up on the road by spooky dancing 'bandits', faces painted white and whisky bottles passing, you should give a banknote or two to the money-tree.

Such public display of pecuniary piety as the money-tree procession builds religious merit for those involved and also increases secular status. Having money, displaying money and giving away money are important marks of status.

Some visitors find this obvious and ubiquitous use of money conflicts with the romantic idea they would like to have of how Thais live. For some reason, the sweet-scented flower garlands lose something of their charm when a hundred baht banknote is ostentatiously clipped to it. But without money there would be no ceremony, no food, no drink and no fun.

Ceremonies, and the reciprocity they involve, maintain Thai communities. Money, instead of destroying social relationships, can help to maintain them. Money is neutral. But the more of it the better.

BIRTH

The precise time of a baby's entry into the world is a key factor in Thai fortune-telling. *Karma* of past lives causes an individual to be reborn

Carrying money-trees and new robes to the Wat.

in a certain situation, in a specific place and at a precise time. For this reason, birth time is noted as accurately as possible and will be used thirty days after birth for the first of many fortune-tellings.

Making a Soul

Soon after birth, the baby is the centre of the *tham khwan sam wan* ceremony. The name means literally 'making a soul (after) three days'. This is the first of many *tham khwan* ceremonies an individual will undergo at important stages in life or whenever he is sick or depressed. On future occasions he will go to a Buddhist monk to request a *tham* (make, (re)make/sustain) *khwan* (spirit matter, soul) but monks play no role in this first ceremony, which is entirely animistic.

The rationale behind this ceremony is that a baby is sent into his mother's womb by a spirit. It is debatable how many Thais actually believe this in these days when family planning and anti-sexually transmitted disease campaigns include such beautiful Thai-isms as monks blessing piles of condoms, campaigners handing out visiting cards which bear the Buddhist scripture, 'Many births cause suffering' and have a brightly coloured contraceptive attached, and the slogan, 'Space your next pregnancy with a pig' (a reference to the free piglet given in some areas of the country to families who practise family planning) and which is sometimes written on a pig!

A young girl who pleads with an angry father that the baby in her womb was sent by a spirit is, these days, likely to be thrashed until she reveals the name of the 'spirit'. Sceptical as they are of 'immaculate conception', many village Thais still prefer not to risk incurring the wrath of the spirit-mother by forgetting to hold the *tham khwan* ceremony. (Although few urban Thais now feel it necessary.)

The three-day-old child is placed on a wicker winnowing tray and rocked gently from side to side, a symbolic separating of 'grain' from 'chaff' and good from bad, while the spirit mother is told 'three days (old) a spirit child, four days a child of man, whoever's child this is come take him'. An old woman (never the mother) then 'buys' the child by offering a coin to the spirit. If the spirit tries to get its child

A village pig advertises, 'I use condoms'.

157

back in the future, it will go to the wrong 'mother'. (Sometimes spirits can be very easily tricked, especially when money is involved!) In the past, but rarely today, the child would have a candle burning above its bed throughout the following month.

Taboos

Pregnant Thai women are traditionally surrounded by many taboos which, among other things, prevent them fishing, eating chillies, telling lies or visiting the sick and attending funerals. Contravention of these taboos puts the baby's health at risk. Although few women would attend a funeral when pregnant, most, in Bangkok at least, are today quite happy to dismiss the stricture against eating chillies as 'silly superstition'. Very few mothers now confine themselves next to a hot stove after childbirth (this was traditionally required for between 7 and 21 days).

First Haircut

If the child survives a month, the parents give a feast for relatives and friends and the baby has its first haircut. This ceremony is called *tham khwan duan*, literally 'making the soul (after) one month'. As with the first, this *tham khwan* protects the newborn from evil spirits, who like to make themselves at home in the hair. More public than the 'three-day' ceremony, it announces to the world that the baby has been born, has survived the most dangerous period of its life, and is ready to be introduced to the Buddhist community.

Three

The magic number 3 is very evident in both of these ceremonies, the first taking place 3 days after birth and the second 30 (in Thai 'three tens') days after birth. This number is also evident in the fact that nine monks are invited to chant from the scriptures at the 30-day ceremony. Nine is clearly 3 x 3; in Thai the pronunciation '*kaw*' means both the number nine and 'to advance' and is therefore specially significant for marking birthdays.

Birthdays

Thais consider every 12th year of life particularly significant and will usually mark it by giving a special party at the house and inviting nine monks to chant. Most important is the 60th birthday, which often marks a withdrawal from the active world.

The visitor should be aware that Thais often invite people to their home on birthdays. They may not mention the reason for celebration when making the invitation, but this may be discovered by asking another guest. No special gifts are required and none are inappropriate. Flowers and fruits are always acceptable on any visit to a Thai home and (Thai) women will often help to prepare food. The woman visitor is not expected to join them, but need not fear insulting her host by bringing along some homemade or shop-purchased cakes.

Please remember that flowers, fruits and Thai cakes are cheap in Bangkok; your gift should therefore be a specially packaged and reasonably expensive presentation. A plastic bag of Thai *khanom*, however delicious, is out, a *farang* cake from a hotel or bakery of repute is definitely in. *Farang* chocolates, in nice boxes, are expensive in Thailand and will be appreciated: they are worth stocking up on during trips overseas.

Naming

A Thai is given his or her name by the parents, who often ask a monk or an elder to select an appropriate one or the first letter or syllable of the name. This name is of two or more syllables and is used for all official/legal purposes. These names are Sanskrit in origin and always have a good meaning (long life, sun, light of happiness etc.). In addition to this 'real' name, almost all Thais possess a nickname, inevitably of one syllable and meaning something like frog, pig, rat, fatty or many variations on tiny.

On significant birthdays, nine monks are invited to chant in the home. Note the practice of chanting with faces hidden behind fans and the white thread carrying 'good vibrations' from the monks to the lay participants. Note also the sideways sitting position of respect.

The use of a nickname is tied up with the idea of avoiding the attention of spirits. Using a person's real name during the first 30 days of life could cause the spirits to focus their attention on the baby, with unfortunate results. Today, most Thais continue to use their nicknames throughout life and many do not know, or ever think to ask, for the real name of their friends.

Compliment-insults
In addition to the use of nicknames, none of which is complimentary in literal translation, babies might be deliberately referred to in disparaging terms. The origin of this practice is the belief that spirits

are attracted to the beautiful. Whether modern Thais believe this or not, it is still possible to hear one mother 'complimenting' another on her *na kliat* (ugly) baby.

This process of compliment-insult suffers in translation and the visitor's natural instinct to compliment parents on their beautiful baby is likely to be understood by anybody who speaks enough English to understand the words spoken. Indeed, it is now common for Thais, particularly the younger generation, to ignore the spirits and compliment in much the same way as *farang* do—although not all *farang* would feel particularly complimented on being told how white and fat their baby is. While being aware of the Thai custom (just in case somebody compliments you on your wretched frog of a child), it is advisable to avoid entering into the spirit of things even if you can say it in Thai. 'Oh my, what an ugly little monster you have', said in English or Thai, is not likely to endear you to the middle-class Thai who spent ten years at Harvard!

It is considered good fortune if a female baby looks like its father and a boy baby looks like its mother. Very frequently one hears Thais say, 'She looks like her father'; even when said straight to the mother it is a compliment combined with something of a blessing. Similarly, telling a father that his son looks like the mother does not cast any doubts on paternity. The visitor, having established the sex of the child, can safely follow this common custom.

PUBERTY

The visitor may be surprised to see some Thai children with their heads closely cropped except for a long topknot. This is done in preparation for the *khon chuk* or 'topknot cutting' ceremony. At this event, the topknot is ceremonially cut off by a Brahmin priest and the child is blessed by Buddhist monks. Relatives and friends are then invited to a *khon chuk* feast.

This ceremony marks the onset of puberty and takes place either in the child's 11th or 13th year, but never in the 12th. The reason for

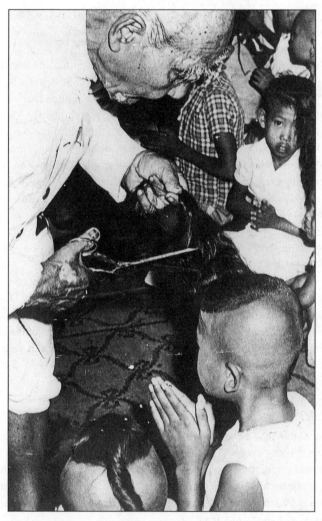

Large numbers of children present themselves at a Royal-sponsored ceremony, held each March, in which topknots are ritually cut by a Brahmin from the Royal Household.

this is usually explained by the belief that odd numbers are lucky whereas even numbers are generally unlucky. However, the 12th year of one's life is not regarded as unlucky. It is the completion of the first 12-year cycle and a time for celebration. The taboo on performing this ceremony during the 12th year may have something to do with the fact that the 12-year calendar was introduced from China, while the *khon chuk* ceremony (like most Thai ceremonies) is of Hindu-Indian origin. (Some 'Brahmin priests' trace their ancestry back for centuries but they are Thais, not Indians. They remain significant in the royal household, but much of their role in popular ceremony is now performed by Buddhist monks.)

The *khon chuk* ceremony is less common today than in the past and many parents do not bother with it unless their child has been sick frequently, in which case a spirit medium might advise that it be performed. It remains sufficiently popular for large numbers of children to present themselves at a Royal-sponsored ceremony for the poor held each March, in which topknots are ritually cut by a Brahmin from the Royal Household.

ORDINATION

Ordination into the Buddhist order of monks is often seen as a ceremony marking entry into the adult world of responsibilities. Most Thai men *Buat Phra* (enter the monkhood) at some point in life, usually just before they get married. Many remain in the monkhood for only a short period, sometimes just a few days, but more often throughout one *Phansa*, the three-month Buddhist Lent which coincides with the rainy season. For this reason, most ordinations take place in July just before *Khao Phansa* (beginning of Lent).

Eligibility

To *Buat Phra*, a man must be at least 20 years old and physically firm and free from contagious disease, must not have killed his parents or a monk, must have obtained his parents' permission and must be free of family and other economic responsibilities. To these traditional requirements a new one has been added: a man must have completed at least four years of schooling.

Motive

The purpose of becoming a monk remains what it has always been: to acquire a deeper knowledge of Buddhist teachings through study, self-deprivation and meditation, to progress along the path to enlightenment (the overcoming of all suffering) and to bring merit to one's parents.

Women

Women cannot become monks and therefore try their best to persuade their sons or husbands to ordain. Thai women do not regard this prohibition as in any way 'sexist', although many may tend to compensate for this natural disability by accumulating as much religious merit as possible; certainly the vast majority of people seen offering food to the monks on the morning almsround are women.

Nuns

Some women become nuns by shaving their heads, wearing white robes and obtaining permission to live in nun's quarters on grounds within the temple. They, too, are fed by the laity but they do not make the almsround. They are supported directly through food, daily requirements and money presented by the lay population to the *Wat*. Their daily routine is as near to that of a monk as it can be, much of their time being spent in study, meditation and counselling of lay people.

Although expected to lead good and celibate lives, nuns are not bound to their vows in the same way as monks and they do not officiate at any ritual activity. During ceremonies they sit with the lay people, not with the monks. Some young girls become nuns for a set

The vast majority of people seen offering food to the monks on the morning almsround are women.

number of days in order to keep a vow made during a period of sickness or to mentally and socially absolve themselves from the result of past bad actions and present problems and misfortunes. Such temporary nuns do not shave their heads.

Nuns must conform to the taboo against females touching a monk or his robes or handing him something directly. This taboo is not extended to nuns—the male or female visitor who wishes to hand something to a nun may do so directly.

Vows

Before a man becomes a monk, he is required to learn by heart the long request for ordination, which he must say in Pali, the language of the

165

scriptures. He should also contemplate the meaning of the 227 rules of conduct a monk is required to keep. The most important of these are the vow of celibacy and the strictures against taking life, eating any food after midday, indulging in magic and taking intoxicants. If any monk feels he can no longer keep his vows, he may request the abbot to release him from them, at which point he returns to lay life.

Sukhwan Nak Ceremony

The ordination ceremony is the most Buddhist of Thai religious rites. It is preceded by a lay ceremony, the *sukhwan nak*, which functions to protect the candidate for ordination from the powers of evil spirits. The candidate is particularly vulnerable to accidents during the period between having the head shaved, which sets him apart from other men, and obtaining the safety of the monastic order. During this period he is known as a *nak*, literally a 'dragon', a name which refers to a Buddhist myth of a dragon who wanted to be a monk. The use of this term emphasises the transitional nature of the candidate who is neither layman nor monk. Perhaps the term functions in the same way as nicknames, to confuse the spirits, who would think twice before attacking a dragon.

The *sukhwan nak* ceremony takes place either in the candidate's home or in the *sala* (community hall) of the *Wat*. If long and elaborate, as it always is for a *phu yai*'s son, it takes place on the evening before ordination. Alternatively, it may precede the ordination service and may sometimes be omitted completely.

The *nak*'s head and eyebrows are shaved as a symbol of repudiation of vanity and sexuality. He is then dressed in white and is the centre of an elaborate ceremony in which no monks participate although they may be present. The *sukhwan nak* is conducted by a professional master-of-ceremonies who together with his assistant sings for up to three or four hours, recounting the pain and suffering of the mother in giving birth and emphasising the importance of fulfilling filial obligations.

At the sukhwan nak ceremony, friends and neighbours give banknotes. These are often attached to flower garlands and hung around the neck of the nak.

This ceremony concludes with all relatives and friends sitting in a circle holding the protective white thread and then passing three sets of three lighted candles in a clockwise direction, an action known as *vientien*. (A different form of *vientien* occurs when, instead of passing the candles, these are carried three times around the outside of the *Bot*, the central sanctuary of the temple, on the occasions of the Buddha's birthday in May and *Khao Phansa* in July.) It is customary for guests to give money, either attached to flower garlands and hung around the neck of the *nak* or deposited on a tray provided.

Ordination Ceremony

The following morning the *nak* is carried on shoulders under tall umbrellas in a colourful procession to the *Bot*. After parading three times around the *Bot*, the *nak* throws coins into the air, an action which

167

The abbot places the sling of the alms bowl over the candidate's head.

symbolises rejection of material pleasures (a rejection eagerly awaited by little boys who scramble for the money), and is carried over the threshold into the *Bot*.

The *nak*, still dressed in white, goes down on his knees in prostration before his father who hands him the saffron robes he will wear as a monk and leads him to the abbot who waits with at least four other monks (usually many more) seated on a raised platform in front of the main Buddha image. After three prostrations to the abbot, the *nak* asks for permission to be ordained. The abbot holds the hand of the *nak*, recites a scripture on the impermanent nature of the human body and places a yellow sash on his body to symbolise acceptance for ordination. The *nak* is then taken out of view and dressed in saffron robes by the two monks who will be responsible for supervising his instruction. He then requests the ten basic vows of a novice monk, repeating each as it is said.

In the past it was usual to spend several years as a novice before full ordination. Today, the prerequisite of four years' education serves the same purpose and the two ceremonies usually follow one immediately after the other.

The father of the candidate presents the alms bowl and other gifts to the abbot, who places the sling of the bowl over the candidate's head to rest on his shoulder. The candidate then stands facing the Buddha and answers questions designed to make sure the basic conditions for entry to the monkhood are upheld. The two 'teacher monks' then request other monks present to accept a new member and give a sermon on the behaviour expected of a monk.

The ceremony concludes with all monks chanting and the new monk pouring water from a silver container into a bowl as a sign that he transfers all merit acquired through being a monk to his parents, who subsequently perform the same rite to transfer some of the merit to their ancestors (who, of course, have been reborn somewhere and benefit from this action). Thus the central ceremony in the life of a Thai man reinforces his identity as Buddhist, cuts him off from his family and marks adult maturity, and at the same time strengthens the link between generations and emphasises the importance of family and community.

MARRIAGE

Choosing Partners

It is perhaps characteristic of the independent nature of the Thais that an individual generally selects his or her marriage partner without too much outside interference. (Although things are moving in this direction throughout Asia, few Asian families allow their children as much freedom as the Thai.) Parents can, however, influence the choice of partner. This seems to be particularly the case among wealthy or influential families, but it is also true that most marriages in the villages tend to take place between members of two families of similar economic and social status. There are no ethnic or religious restrictions and intermarriage is common, particularly between Thai girls and *farang* men.

Types of Marriage

Wedding ceremonies vary between the very elaborate and the non-existent. A couple may be fully recognised as husband and wife simply by living together for a time and having children. Thus, people can become 'gradually married' without any fuss or ceremony (and, just as easily, become gradually divorced!). However, most parents prefer their children to have some kind of ceremony and within the upper echelons of society an elaborate and expensive wedding ceremony is essential.

Thais are legally required to register marriages at the district office, although there is no penalty for failing to do so and many do not. Only one legal marriage is allowed at a time. A well-off man may, however, have several *mia noy* (minor wives). *Mia noy* have no legal rights, but their children are recognised as legitimate under Thai law. Divorce is easy for either party to a marriage and requires only that both sign a statement of mutual consent at the district office. If only one party seeks divorce, it is necessary to demonstrate desertion or non-provision of maintenance for one year. The divorce rate, official and unofficial, is high by any standards and divorce is usually followed by remarriage.

Wedding Ceremony

Wedding ceremonies are usually held, if at all, only to mark the first marriage. The two families agree beforehand on the expenses of the ceremony and the 'bride price' to be paid. The wedding day begins with the couple feeding the monks in the early morning and receiving their blessings. A procession of gifts from the house of the groom to that of the bride was usual in the past but is less frequently seen today.

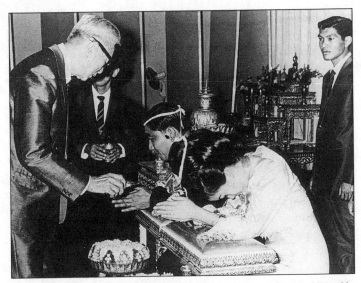

Heads linked with joined loops of sai monkon, a couple's marriage is blessed by a respected elder who pours water over the hands of the bride and groom.

The wedding consists of the couple kneeling side by side, the groom to the right of the bride. At an auspicious time, chosen by an astrologer or a monk, their heads are linked with joined loops of *sai monkon* (white thread) by a senior elder who then pours sacred water over the hands of the couple. The water drips from their hands into bowls of ornately arranged flowers. Guests then bless the couple by pouring water in the same fashion.

Monks may be present, but the Thai wedding ceremony is essentially non-religious and no vows are made to love and cherish (and certainly not to obey!) until 'death do us part'. It may be significant that the white thread that usually unites everybody in a single circle is, in the wedding ceremony, formed into two linked but independent circles. Individual identity is retained but destinies are linked.

Variations on the basic ceremony are many. Certainly, most weddings are much shorter and less elaborate than in the past. In many rural areas the 'sympathetic magic' of having an old couple, evidence of a successful marriage, 'prepare the bridal bed' continues to be practised. This semi-farce requires the jolly couple to lie on the bed before the newlyweds and chatter away saying lots of auspicious things like 'This bed seems very lucky to me, I think whoever sleeps on it will have lots of children and be rich …'

The old couple then get off the bed and place on it many symbols of fertility and prosperity including a tomcat, bags of rice, sesame seeds and coins, a stone pestle, and a bowl of rainwater. The newlyweds should share their bed with these objects (but not the tomcat!) for three days, which probably explains why most middle-class couples today prefer to leave after the wedding party for a honeymoon in Phuket!

The Inevitable

If you do manage to find excuses to stay on in this wonderland of a country, and learn some Thai, you will become very used to the question, 'Married already or not yet?' It is always asked in this way. There is no possibility of escaping the event, it's simply a question of when. If you are unmarried, you are obliged to answer 'not yet'. This is really the only answer possible in Thai, even if you are a confirmed homosexual. With time, the repeated 'not yet' begins to sound somewhat deviant, particularly if you are 39 years old.

Finally, you bow to the will of the majority and tie the circles with a Thai. You will still be asked, 'Married already or not yet?' but now, a responsible human being at last, you can answer proudly 'Married already.' The pride will last just until the next question, 'Have children or not yet?' And when you do have three little children climbing over you as you wait in the maternity hospital for the fourth to be delivered, the chap next to you will ask, 'What your name?' 'How old are you?' and 'Married already or not yet?'

DEATH

Of all life cycle rites, Thais consider the *ngarn sop* (cremation ceremony) to be the most important. Funeral rites mark not only the end of a life, but the start of a journey towards rebirth. Death is seen as a transition, a natural and necessary part of life.

Rebirth

If an individual is seriously ill, friends and relatives will help him to direct the mind to the Buddha and Buddha's teachings. This provides the dying with psychological comfort by preparing his mind for a good rebirth.

Belief in reincarnation is essential to the Thai view of life and religion, which maintains that an individual's material existence is determined by a spiritual balance of all of his or her good and bad actions (*karma*) and that the course of existence, in this life and the next, can be changed by making religious merit (*tham boon*). Because of the importance of these 'rites of passage' from one life to another, they are usually as elaborate as a dead person's relatives and friends can afford.

Preparing the Corpse

After death, the corpse is bathed by members of the family, perfumed, dressed in new clothes and laid out on a mat. Relatives and friends line up to bless the departed soul by pouring water over the right hand of the dead body.

A one baht coin is placed in the mouth (to enable the dead to buy his way into purgatory), the hands are placed together in a *wai* and tied with white thread. Between the palms are placed a banknote, two flowers and two candles. The ankles are also tied with thread, the mouth and eyes are sealed with wax and the corpse is placed in a coffin with the head pointing towards the west, the direction of the setting sun and of death.

Family members carry a picture of the deceased and monks lead the funeral procession to the crematorium. Behind the coffin walk the men of the village, and behind them, the women.

At the head of the coffin a lamp is kept burning to help the soul find its way to the west. Near it are placed personal objects such as the deceased's sleeping mat, blanket, plates, food and clothing and a knife, for use in purgatory.

Visitors help family members to prepare the funeral feast and make merit by giving a small banknote to the family. These notes are often fixed on bamboo sticks and planted like flags into the sides of the coffin.

During the three days following death, monks receive their morning meal from the family of the deceased and chant in the house. In small villages with only one or two monks, messengers are sent out to neighbouring villages to invite monks to attend the funeral. The presence of monks is essential.

The Funeral

The coffin is carried out of the house feet-first. In rural households built on stilts, the jar of drinking water outside the house is turned upside down and the house ladder is reversed in a symbolic negation of the world of the living to discourage the ghost from returning home.

Family members, carrying a picture of the deceased, a tray of tinder to start the funeral pyre and a jar in which the remains will be collected, lead the funeral procession to the crematorium. Behind them, monks, walking in pairs (for funerals only), hold the sacred white thread which is fastened to the foot of the coffin. Behind the coffin walk the men of the village and behind the men, the women. Rice is scattered to placate the many spirits attracted to funeral activities.

On arriving at the *Wat*, the coffin is carried three times around the crematorium (which was in the past and still is in remote rural areas, an open funeral pyre). The usual practice of clockwise circumambulation is reversed on this occasion, continuing the symbolic negation made at the start of the funeral procession. Coconut water is then poured onto the face of the corpse by a pair of monks who are followed by a long queue of relatives and villagers who bless the dead by pouring scented water onto the body.

The string is detached from the foot of the coffin and fastened at its head. Monks chant the *suadnitcha*, which tells of the inevitability of suffering and death as the white cloth (symbolising death) is lifted from the coffin by the most senior monk present, the coffin is placed into the crematorium or onto the pyre, and the body is consumed in flames.

It is customary to hold a funeral feast in the *Wat* grounds. Everybody is welcome. Guests avoid bright colours, and relatives wear black and white, the colours of mourning, but this feast is not a sad occasion.

That evening, and for the following two evenings, monks will come to the house of the dead person to chant the *suad paritta monkhon* to bless the departed soul and protect the living. Chantings are followed by parties, open to all visitors, when people eat, drink and play games with the direct intention of making family members happy. There is no reason to be sad; the departed is advancing along the great cycle of death and rebirth towards the ultimate state of existence, the state of perfect peace.

> *In this world everything changes*
> *except good deeds and bad deeds;*
> *these follow you as the shadow*
> *follows the body.*

ABSORBING THE SHOCK

THE HUMAN TRANSPLANT

Culture is a particular way of doing things. All people everywhere eat, talk, play, work and think; but not all people eat the same thing the same way, talk the same language, play the same games, do the same work or think the same thoughts. All people have families, places to live, tools, weapons and clothing; but not all people recognise the same boundaries to the family, live in the same type of place, use the same tools and weapons and wear the same clothes.

Human society is divided into an infinite series of cultures and subcultures, all of which overlap and interact like ripples on the water. Cultural differences are always sufficient to allow any group of people to see itself as different from others. However, the similarities between human cultures mean that no matter how great the differences, these can always be translated and understood between cultures. (With time, patience and plenty of smiles ...)

Cultural Transplant

When a liver, kidney or heart is transplanted into a different body from the one it grew in, a period of adjustment is followed by acceptance or rejection of the transplanted part. The visitor to Thailand is in much the same situation. He is a cultural transplant, and the degree to which he is accepted or rejected depends on how well he can fit into his new surroundings.

The initial impact of Thailand and Thai culture is likely to make the transplanted visitor very conscious of himself and the world he left behind. He will try to translate what he sees, hears, smells and feels into concepts with which he is familiar. When he is unable to make an adequate translation, he becomes confused, cannot function properly, and veers wildly between love and hate for his new surroundings. It is at this point that the transplant is most at risk. This is the period when the transplant experiences CULTURE SHOCK.

At the risk of simplicity, we feel all transplants experience something of two contradictory feelings: disgust and rapture.

The Disgusted

Some people feel culture shock in the popular, literal sense of the term. They are shocked and disgusted by the world in which they find themselves. No sooner are they through the glass doors at the airport, when they are surrounded by 'Hey you, where you go, you wan taxi?' The taxi meter which doesn't work; the impossibly crowded buses; the toilet with nowhere to sit; the used toilet paper staring at you from the basket; the English or lack of it; the Thai inability to read a map of Bangkok or give directions more specific than 'over there'; the nostrils cleared without a handkerchief; the non-drinkable water; the heat, the noise, the dirt, the flies, mosquitoes, ants, spiders, lizards and snakes. Even the chicken soup has a chicken's foot floating in it. 'Oh, what am I doing here? Why did I ever come to this country?'

All of this has very little to do with Thai culture. Apart from the chicken's foot soup, Thais dislike most of it almost as much as the visitor. But, being Thais, they avoid it or ignore it. Thais have a gift for being able to ignore anything they don't try too hard to notice.

Once out of the tourist/girly-bar environment, most of the hassle disappears. Some things which don't disappear just have to be lived with. You will soon learn to squat on the toilet and to pack an emergency supply of toilet paper along with your toothbrush when going 'upcountry'. Most people find they eventually adapt to most things—with a little help from mosquito repellents and air-conditioners!

The real tragedy is that although there have been very significant improvements in amenities, many short-term visitors receive an impression of Thailand that is largely negative and completely wrong. They may have spent a few days in Bangkok, but they haven't been to Thailand.

The Enrapt

Other visitors feel culture shock in a very different way. They fall madly in love with the cultural differences around them. Usually, the enrapt focus on a completely different part of life in Thailand to that experienced by the disgusted. The peaceful monks, the fantastic temples, the festivals and ceremonies, Thai dancing and handicrafts, the smiling, goodnatured people. 'Oh, how beautiful everything and everybody is.'

The enrapt view of Thailand is infinitely more acceptable to the Thais than the opinion of the disgusted, but it is equally false and ethnocentric. Thailand, and the Thais, could never be as nice as the enrapt would like to think they are. Some of the enrapt manage to stay in Thailand for years without adjusting their romantic image of the Thais, but many others fall victim to depression and disillusionment as soon as they realise that these 'wonderful, beautiful people' are really quite human after all. Beautiful, charming and tolerant, yes they are; saints they are not (and never pretend to be).

There is nothing wrong with telling Thais how beautiful everything is, since that is what they want to hear, but don't believe it too much, at least not 100 per cent. You might get hurt.

The Puzzled

Most visitors to Thailand, especially those with the prospect of spending some time here, feel very much like fish out of water when they first arrive. In a strange world, never quite sure what is going on, never sure what is the right thing to do, never sure if people approve or disapprove, surrounded by signs that can't be read, a language that doesn't make sense, strange food, strangers with strange customs. One moment enrapt with the beauty of it all, the next moment disgusted with it all. And most of the time, puzzled.

One of the paradoxes of the twentieth century is that a man can be uprooted, flown halfway around the world, dropped down in another time, climate and culture, and expect to get up the following day and function as usual. Like a rice seedling torn from its protected nursery and transplanted in a big, strange field.

Like the fragile seedling, the human transplant must either adapt and flourish or wither and perish. But unlike the pampered seedling, the man must survive without the loving care of the farmer and without the company of other seedlings of the same stock.

It is a great tribute to the human race that most people in this position do manage to carry on somehow. Indeed, many of them revel in the novelty of their situation. But all feel at least something of the disorientation of culture shock.

A Child Again

The newcomer finds himself suddenly unsure of when and how to go about the basic and 'natural' actions of daily life. He doesn't even know when to say 'good morning'. He may react by saying a hundred 'good mornings' to any Thai around him, when he made do with two or three back home. He doesn't know when it is appropriate to shake hands, give tips, talk to strangers, make invitations, refuse invitations. He has very little idea of what to say when he meets people, even if they speak his language, doesn't know what is funny and what is serious, and has no idea what people are thinking. Nothing seems to have a pattern and he finds it almost impossible to predict what will be happening and how he will be feeling from one hour to the next. He is a child again.

Grown responsible adults suddenly find themselves back in infancy. Like children they must rely on others, Thais who speak a few words of their language, for the simplest of things. Making phone calls, catching a bus, buying a packet of cigarettes and posting a letter become adventures; finding a place to live and hiring a maid become major preoccupations, and doing the shopping becomes an expedition. Like the world of children, the new world of Thailand is unknown, exciting and potentially dangerous.

Unfortunately for the foreign visitor, the Thais, ultra-tolerant as they are, do not extend childhood status to visiting adults. Young children, Thai or foreign, can do more or less as they like for several years and get away with almost anything; the adult visitor cannot.

During a very short period of time you must make essential adjustments to your behaviour and learn to reinterpret the world around you in a somewhat different way. The psychological pressure involved in attempting to adapt to two interpretations of the world can result in a feeling of euphoria in the morning and depression in the afternoon. The Thais are basically nice people (we think) and they (almost) certainly won't mind you smiling, giggling and laughing when the euphoria strikes; but cry and you cry alone.

THE VISITOR STRIKES BACK

The state of disequilibrium and confusion which characterises the initial period of culture shock does not last long. Human beings hate being strangers, being 'left out', and feeling helpless. Thus, very soon, the visitor strikes back. Seeking to defend his senses against the shock-waves of an alien world, he searches for, or tries to construct, a culture shock absorber.

In order to retain some sanity, the visitor responds to culture shock in one or all of the following four ways: escape, confrontation, encapsulation, integration.

Escape

Escape is the easiest way out. Short-term visitors who know they can 'escape' in a few days or weeks are free to enjoy their culture shock experience to the full. Good luck to them.

Other foreigners we have met, working in Thailand for a year or more, also respond by escape. They escape from the Thai world in which they feel uncomfortable, into their own homes, eat familiar imported food, watch satellite television and mix socially with expats or foreign educated Thais. 'Living in Thailand, and all the problems this involves, is temporary; it is not worth trying to overcome the problems because in one or two years we will be leaving.' Full blown escapees are mentally always in the transit lounge.

Confrontation

Some visitors are always complaining—mostly to other visitors who feel the same way, but sometimes to Thais. Stated or implied in their criticisms of Thai values and behaviour is an assumption that things are better where they come from. Not-too-deep-down-inside they enjoy feeling superior to the world around them. They make sense; the Thai world 'doesn't make sense'. For these visitors, Thai culture is there to fight against and to succeed in spite of.

Encapsulation

All foreigners, to a varying extent, retreat into a 'culture bubble' made up of people facing common problems in an alien culture. They become a part of the 'community of travellers' or of the 'expat community'. The culture to which they adjust is the lowest common denominator of many different parts: a culture of transplants. There are expat clubs, shops and supermarkets catering for the English-speaking, expat doctors, expat sports, expat schools for expat children. Expats, whether from America, Japan, Africa or neighbouring Asia, meet on the cocktail circuits and invite each other to their houses. A community of strangers in paradise, where the like-situated rub shoulders and where most of the Thais in the room are there to serve the drinks, clear away the food and sweep the floor.

Belonging to a club because it shows movies you like and sending your children to an English-medium school, etc. is only normal, human behaviour. This very human grouping together to pursue a common goal need not exclude all the benefits of the Thai world. Comparatively few foreigners in Thailand are completely encapsulated. Many find they grow out of (or bored with) the expat situation as soon as they have found their feet in the new environment.

Integration

Integration means to fit together; to abolish segregation through the removal of social barriers that divide members of different cultures.

The non-Thai visitor has a good chance of integrating with Thais, if this is what he wants. In doing so, he will retain his original cultural identity and the Thais will maintain theirs. Integration is not assimilation; the visitor has practically no chance of really 'becoming Thai', however much he loves Thailand and however long he lives here.

For integration to take place, the visitor consciously or unconsciously removes the social barriers that cut him off from Thais. This is usually a slow process. The foreigner finds himself decreasingly relying on the foreign community in Bangkok for friendships and entertainment and feels increasingly at ease with Thais.

Integration takes place to a varying degree with most visitors who stay some time. It gives the best of both worlds. When the barriers are down, one's own culture can be enjoyed every bit as much as the new host culture. The individual has everything to gain and little to lose but intolerance (and, of course, culture shock).

Removing the Barriers

Removing social barriers is a lot more difficult than it sounds. If you are working in Thailand, you are likely to be constantly expected and even required (by fellow expats and by Thais) to live up to the role demanded by 'expat culture'.

'Life is tiring enough, who has time and energy to reach out to the Thai community more than is absolutely necessary or immediately enjoyable?' The only answer to this question, repeated in one form or another by most expats we interviewed before beginning this book, is that we know coming to live and work in Thailand is tiring, at least initially, but getting to understand something about the Thais is likely to make it less tiring. By all means begin your personal study of the Thais with whatever you find immediately enjoyable, be it the massage parlour or Thai classical dancing; as you learn more about the Thais, many other aspects of their culture might attract you.

Absorbing the Shock

If you do have the time and opportunity, the following programme will minimise the negative aspects of culture shock and permit you to enjoy Thailand from the beginning.

1. If possible, take a cultural orientation course before leaving home, although very few foreign companies offer such courses to their employees before sending them to Thailand. If there is no chance of a course, try at least to read some books before you leave (at the very least, this one!).

2. Learn as quickly as possible the basic do's and don'ts set out in this book. For the really busy and tired, these are listed in easy reference form at the back.

3. Learn the language. This will remove some of the communication barrier and teach you a lot about Thai culture. There are many private tutors in Bangkok who will fit their hours to your convenience. Better, if you have the time, is to attend the intensive courses at the AUA on Rajdamri Road. There, apart from language laboratories and an experienced teaching staff, you will have the psychological prop of learning a difficult language in a small group of foreigners, all of whom find things just as difficult. Since the Thai course is an appendage to what is essentially an English language school for Thais, the minute you leave the classroom you are in a Thai-speaking environment, with lots of pleasant young people who have nothing much to do and will talk to you, preferably in Thai, for as long as you can stand it.

4. Read what you can about Thailand and the Thais, bearing in mind that a great deal of it has been written by *farang* obviously enrapt by it all. An annotated bibliography is to be found at the back of this book which should get you started on the mass of English language literature on Thailand. If in Bangkok for a time, request permission to use the AUA library on Rajdamri. When you find yourself developing an interest in Thailand, you might decide to graduate to the Siam Society and its wide ranging library on Soi Asoke (you have to be a member). For the really hooked, or for those looking for specific information, the Thailand Information Centre in Chulalongkorn University has most things written on the country and an excellent subject index to help you find what you are looking for (if you don't find what you want there, bear in mind that it takes a year or two for new stuff to get indexed and ask the staff).

5. Take any of the English-language evening lecture courses on various aspects of Thailand (usually art or history), advertised

periodically in the *Bangkok Post*. The Siam Society and the AUA also have interesting one-off lectures from time to time.

6. Whenever you are tempted to criticise the Thais, remember that you are a transplanted foreign part in a culture that is very different to the one you are used to. Full acceptance by the host culture will take some time and involve changes in you rather than it. Being a transplant is physically and mentally tiring, so take it easy, don't try to become Thai overnight. (After twenty years in the country, maybe …)

Culture Shock Relapse

Coming out of culture shock is not a simple lineal process. Within a few days, weeks or months, depending on your personality and past experience of other cultures, you will get to find your way around and cope with the obvious differences. The agony and ecstasy of culture shock is felt less intensely. You come to terms with being a foreigner. All around you, Thai is spoken and written; it remains unintelligible, but you have got used to it and it doesn't bother you any more.

After several months or years more, just as you think you are beginning to understand what being Thai is all about … culture shock relapse. A person to whom you have never spoken will send the servant with a basket of mangoes as a present for you; your trusted maid will go away for two days to visit her mother and never return. Once again, it doesn't make sense.

Learning Culture

In many ways, as you get to know more about Thais, the stranger they seem and the stranger *you* seem. When you have come to think of somewhere as 'home', it is very disturbing to be suddenly reminded that you are a foreigner. But try not to get too depressed about culture shock relapses, they are all part of the learning process.

Whenever culture shock strikes, in whatever form, and however euphoric or depressed it makes you feel, try to remember that the basic

ingredient of culture shock is ignorance; a situation arises and you don't know how to act, once you have learnt to understand the situation from a Thai point of view, culture shock just fades away.

All culture is learnt. Anybody, given enough time, patience and motivation, can learn any culture.

COUNTING THE COSTS

First Meeting

Bangkok is by no means all there is to Thailand, but for most foreign visitors it is their first impression of the Thai world, and whether we like it or not (and we don't), their first meeting with Thai culture.

Urbanisation and Westernisation are now as much a part of Bangkok-Thai culture as the *wai* and the *Wat*. Certainly, the culture of modern Bangkok is likely to relate much more to a visitor's initial culture shock than anything included in the tourist guides. To ignore Bangkok would be to ignore that part of Thailand's culture in which most visitors spend a large amount of their time.

Every Taboo Broken

In Bangkok, the visitor will see every taboo broken. Young girls swing braless along the street, hand in hand with a (usually foreign) boyfriend. Small men pretending to be big men talk loudly and rudely in restaurants. The waitress in Patpong Road looks askance at your *wai*-deserving tip and flips over her tray to show you the words CHEAPSKATE CHARLIE. We could, unfortunately, go on and on.

The fact that deviancy is evident publicly does not mean that Thai society does not value correct (i.e., Thai) behaviour. The great (silent) majority of the Thai population dislike bad behaviour and avoid the company of those who go in for it. Nobody would deny that Westernisation and urbanisation are rapidly taking place but, even in Bangkok, Thai ways of doing things are still very relevant.

To repeat ourselves: the visitor should model his behaviour on the generally acceptable rather than the exceptional. One good reason for doing so is that the Thai population, used to hearing how decadent foreigners have corrupted Thai youth, love a foreigner who can show he knows how to behave.

City of Angels

Bangkok's Thai name, Krung Thep, means 'city of angels'. Of course, the city was given this name a long time before it became famous for its bars and prostitution and infamous for its crime rate, noise level and traffic congestion.

Bangkok is a hot, humid, dirty, noisy and congested city. But the angels are still here, amid it all. Calm Thai faces packed together on a Bangkok bus crawling through the black smoke of a seemingly perpetual slow-motion rush hour.

First Impressions

The first reaction of the visitor to this new world is likely to be bewilderment and even horror. 'Culture shock' in the fullest and ugliest sense of the term. Foreign tourists, long-term expats and Thais agree completely that Bangkok is hot, humid, dirty, noisy and congested. The strange thing is that very few Thais living here can ever be persuaded to live anywhere else and the visitors seem very reluctant to leave.

Second Impressions

Second impressions are not much better. New arrivals inevitably find that their centrally located hotel seems to be near nowhere they want to go. Old arrivals working in Thailand complain that whichever Ministry of Foreign Affairs they go to, it is always the wrong one and when they drive across to the other one, it is also the wrong one. Visitors to UNICEF on the river who also want to visit UNESCO have to travel right across town to the outer reaches of Sukhumvit. Everybody complains that there is no 'downtown', no city centre, 'things are spread all over the place'. One poetic newcomer we spoke to had formerly worked in India. He quoted Rudyard Kipling's impression of Calcutta and suggested it would be more appropriately applied to Bangkok:

> As fungus sprouts chaotic from its bed;
> So it spread;
> Chance directed,
> Chance erected, so they built;
> On the silt.

Third Impressions

First and second impressions are none too kind. But, before you snap shut this book and, in true Bangkok style, flee the scene, let us assure you that many people who at first hate Bangkok grow to love it. Because of the people, the most positive factor in what may, at least at first, seem to be a largely negative world. In Thailand, third impressions are often the best.

Counting the Costs

If the visitor stays on in Thailand and learns to live with the Bangkok traffic, pollution, heat, mosquitoes, floods, droughts, crippling slowness of bureaucracy and multivariant hazards to life and limb, he will quickly discover that Bangkok is not the price-heaven he thought it would be.

Orchids are Cheap

Certainly Bangkok and Thailand have some bargains, and the average visitor will enjoy pleasures that would cost a fortune or be unavailable back home. Hotel rooms, massage parlours and restaurants are cheap by international standards (but getting less cheap all the time). Cinemas must rate among the cheapest and most comfortable in the world (even if Thai movies, with no subtitles, are not to everybody's taste). A bottle of Thai Mekhong whisky costs one-third the price of Scotch and a bowl of delicious monosodium-glutamate-noodles to go with it can be had with the small change. An exciting ride on a Bangkok bus will take you just about anywhere in town for a song and a prayer. And while hanging out of the doorway you can pick up a bunch of orchids from a street corner vendor for a tiny fraction of what you would pay back home.

So much for the bargains. Thailand is a great place to visit and a great place to live in, if we can judge from the number of *farang* absconders who are obviously here until the *Suad Phra Aphitham* accompanies them to purgatory. But it is not so cheap to live here for long and maintain the same style of life you had back home. This is because much of what you thought of as basic essentials there, are regarded as extravagant luxuries here and taxed accordingly. You can't live on orchids alone.

Cornflakes are Expensive

The American Chamber of Commerce for Thailand surprised a lot of people when it ranked Bangkok as a more expensive place to live in than Washington D.C. They back their statement with lots of figures which should be carefully noted by potential 'expats'. Rent is cheaper outside Bangkok, but everything else is likely to be even more expensive. Average rent on a townhouse in Bangkok (one that is not flooded for two months of the year!) they say is more than twice the going rate in Washington. A new car, a refrigerator and most electrical appliances, including air-conditioners, can cost up to three times the Washington price in Bangkok.

Petrol, electricity, toiletries, toys and all imported foods and products available in 'English-language' supermarkets are likely to cost much more than you would pay back home. And if all this depressing news is enough to drive you to drink, you should be aware that although Thai whisky is comparatively cheap, a bottle of beer in Thailand is comparatively expensive and even drinking-water must be purchased by the bottle.

The visitor is not obliged to live up to the standard of the American Chamber of Commerce. The married man with a family can expect to find a modest house with garden for much less than twice the Washington price if he follows some of the tips set out in Chapter 8, looks around and is not set on living in the heart of the expat community. An apartment costs about the same as a small house (however, it is said to be safer!). If you are single and thinking of staying at least three months, you can rent a comfortable little 'bed-sitting-room' with bathroom, fridge, air-conditioner and all laundry, electricity, water and maid services included for a price which is very reasonable compared to other capital cities, in the Ploenchit/Withayu/Silom/Sathorn area, which is near to where many foreigners want to be and 'central', if anything is.

Servants

One thing that goes some way towards compensating for the high price of baked beans and Vichy water is the ability to buy up large quantities of one comparatively cheap and attractive commodity—human beings.

The rapid economic development of the 1990s and the existence of economic alternatives means servants are no longer knocking on the door begging to clean your house, wash your clothes, go to the market and cook your food. Now you have to look for them and treat them much better. Young people often prefer the freedom of working in a factory with evenings and weekends off. The time when a servant worked hard for a daily wage less than the cost of your breakfast cornflakes is not so far in the past but is gone for good. Still, the chances are you will be able to afford one or more servants, a luxury you probably could not think about back home. And a good maid can greatly improve your life and might even save you money.

The expensive supermarket will sell you exorbitantly priced petit pois in battered tins that have been in the hold of a ship for months, but your servant will buy fresh vegetables for you every day at a fraction of the cost—even if the champignon are a different shape to the ones you had back home.

Morality

While most visitors find it completely acceptable to their preconceptions of morality that servants should be employed to wash clothes, sweep the floor and sit outside all night to guard their property, many draw the line at hiring a temporary wife, even if she is much younger and prettier than the one who took the children back home for the sake of their education. Many others find this one of the most interesting aspects of their stay.

Using People

Some westerners feel uneasy about using other people to do jobs they don't want to do themselves. Some even get indignant at the sight of a row of servants on their knees, moving slowly across the rich man's lawn, cutting the grass with scissors. Such scenes may offend your view of what constitutes human dignity. Few Thais would agree with you.

This first stage of servant culture shock does not last long. At first you will worry about your servant. You might even insist on doing much of the housework yourself—at first. But, surprisingly soon, you are likely to be grumbling with your foreign friends about how your servant lacks all initiative and must be shown every little thing to be done. Then you begin to wonder how she can use so much detergent and whether she really feeds the dog when you go to Pattaya for the weekend.

Status

In spite of their grumblings and costs which increase year by year, most foreigners thoroughly enjoy having servants. It's not just that the dirty jobs get done, it's something more. Having servants, you feel, raises your status. This sudden elevation is the second stage of servant culture shock. It is almost as ethnocentric as the first.

The Thai secretary, bank clerk, schoolteacher or shopkeeper, with a few baht more than barely necessary to get by, will certainly have a servant. Because almost everybody has servants, having them doesn't do much for the ego. The really high-up and wealthy Thai might buy, and show off at any opportunity, the washing machine, vacuum cleaner and floor polisher that the visitor left behind back home. The more they cost, the more status possession represents. The fact that these toys would be operated by servants is a very secondary consideration in status building.

Writing back home that you have one or two servants might make you feel like a little Lord Jim for a while, but it won't impress the Thais much.

After some time, your views on the servant phenomena are likely to approach the Thai perspective. You have the money, so you pay somebody to work for you. Along with the work, you also purchase the right to superficial actions of respect from the servant. These actions simply confirm the obvious, that you are superior to your servant. Having got to this point of view, you can relax when the servant is around. By all means 'befriend' him or her, but maintain appropriate respect procedures.

Social Costs

The Thailand experience affects most visitors in some way for the rest of their lives. All learn at least as much about themselves as they do about the Thais, and while most people appreciate the gift of this knowledge, some find they are confronted by a 'Mr Hyde' they would have preferred to leave in the subconscious.

The technician, schoolteacher or businessman, members of a humble middle-class back home, become incredibly wealthy and privileged individuals in Thailand. You can buy most of your wildest fancies. No budgetary limitations and an apparently endless supply of whatever is desired. In this new situation, preconceived but untested ideas on what constitutes morality often disappear during the first night on the town.

In Thailand some people find themselves and some people lose themselves. For every foreigner taking vows of celibacy as a Buddhist monk, another foreigner is locked away for a long, long prison term for drug trafficking.

Back home, indulgence in sex and drugs was limited, partly at least because they were unavailable. Take a five-minute walk through certain parts of Bangkok and you can refuse both a hundred times. Even the missionary will be tempted.

All this temptation will certainly appeal to many young foreign men, who may feel that they are 'really living' for the first time in their lives. But it doesn't help stabilise marriages or personalities.

The potential expat couple should be aware that the chances of divorce after a couple of years in Thailand (or any other foreign country) are much higher than if they had stayed at home. Marital problems that might lie dormant at home, where husbands and wives can pass the toast to each other every morning for years and stay together while largely ignoring each other, have a habit of leaping to the surface once abroad.

Coming to Thailand frees you from the social restrictions of family, neighbourhood and friends (pressures which may be weaker in industrialised countries than in countries like Thailand but which, even so, assert a sobering influence on behaviour) and at the same time gives you every opportunity to indulge yourself in the temporary pleasures of life.

Many visitors don't think twice before succumbing to temptation. Reasonable enough; the Thais behave in much the same way. But while most Thais would enjoy, discreetly, and forget, some foreigners can't help feeling guilty about their fun. If you are one of them, by all means talk things through with a sympathetic foreign friend, but do not bother a Thai. If you enjoy yourself in this way, the Thai will avoid noticing the fact. But if you tell him or her what you are doing, the Thai might avoid you. Especially if you try to blame Thai society for your decadence.

For the expat, problems within the family are not limited to those caused by misbehaviour (usually of the husband). Almost as destructive is the expat lifestyle. The husband spends long hours at work, often finding much more satisfaction with his job than he did back home. The wife, on the other hand, loses any financial or social independence. The husband is the 'big frog', the wife's status is a reflection of his. The fact that the wife now has servants, a big house, and freedom to pursue other interests or spend more time with the children is not always compensation enough for losing independence of identity.

Children possibly have the most to gain from the expat life. A brave new world of adventure, visible evidence at an impressionable age that there is not just one way of doing things, exposure to experiences friends back home would only see on television, a climate of perpetual summer and caring servants to pamper every caprice.

Not surprisingly, some of these very privileged children are arrogant little monsters. Most, however, grow up to be independent, tolerant and, perhaps surprisingly, more attached to their parents than the kids back home.

The social and economic costs and benefits of living in Thailand as a foreigner are largely the same as those of any expat worker in any culture which is not his own. Whether the positive factors outnumber the negative is really for the individuals involved to decide. At the risk of oversimplification, it may help this decision if we list the balance of these factors in tabular form. If you are thinking of working in Thailand (or any other overseas posting) and you, or a member of your family, feel you couldn't cope with any of the negative factors, perhaps you should think again.

Learning about Thai culture will not remove all of the negative factors involved, but it will focus your mind on the positive aspects of living in Thailand. As long as you feel that you are gaining more than you are losing, you will enjoy your stay.

We are very happy to be able to conclude this section by stating that most foreigners do, on the whole, think positively about Thailand and, weighing up the merits of their time in this country, have no hesitation in declaring a mighty surplus of pleasure over pain.

So, if you are hesitant about the Thailand experience when you first arrive and if your first impressions of Bangkok are the kind you would rather forget, you will (hopefully and before too long) come to realise that Thailand (even Bangkok) does have a heart. A cool heart, not worn on the sleeve. A Thai heart that may not be immediately evident as you step out of the aircraft, but one which might well go on beating when Paris, New York, Moscow, Beijing and Timbuktoo are all dust in a Martian's museum. If you weep on arrival, you are likely to weep even more on departure, and for quite different reasons.

TO EXPAT OR NOT TO EXPAT?

+ *factors*	− *factors*
travel/new experiences/broadening of the mind	losing touch with the world back home/difficulty of fitting in on return
new friends	separation from old friends
a more challenging and responsible job	long hours, many of them 'unproductive'
flattery and temptation from opposite sex	problems with spouse/marital breakdown
fewer financial restrictions/more money/exoticism within your means	(too?) ready availability of sex, drugs and alcohol/high cost of apples, etc.
servants to do the work/more meaningful time with the children	problems with servants/boredom/feeling of 'wasting time'
children 'learn through being' about a wider world	the arrogant expat child phenomenon
children tend to be closer to parents	children away at home for education
great boost to the ego of being different, wealthy and/or white	strain of always being the one who has to adjust to the host culture
stimulant effects of culture shock	depressive effects of culture shock

— *Chapter Eight* —

SETTLING IN

We are fully aware that the newly arrived visitor, gripped as he may be by the more 'cultural' aspects of Thai culture, is likely to be most immediately interested in finding somewhere to live, getting around, and acquiring some basic knowledge about where things are and how things work. This chapter offers some tips for the newcomer.

ACCOMMODATION

In looking for a house or flat check:
1. Noise level (traffic during weekday rush hours, neighbours' children during non-school hours, construction work nearby).

2. Time travelling to work *at the time you would be travelling.*
3. Water: does it flow all day? Is pressure adequate? Is there an annoying and noisy pump?
4. Does the roof leak or the area flood (difficult to check in the dry season, ask the neighbours). Maximum flood time is October but some places are semi-flooded for months.
5. Security: bars on all windows, door locks, guard. Some streets have community guards to which you contribute money.
6. Mosquito screens on all windows.
7. Telephone: waiting to have one installed can take a year or more.
8. What the price includes: furniture, telephone, garbage collection, maid service, repairs, electricity ... In Bangkok expect to get air-conditioner(s), refrigerator and a reasonable kitchen. Services are normally not included. You can ask for furniture to be added at the landlord's expense.

Prices are, as in most developing capitals, going up all the time. If inclined, you might consider the merits of purchasing an apartment in a condominium; otherwise it is not legal for a foreigner to purchase property or land in Thailand. The legal right for foreigners to purchase a residence is under review; check with a solicitor if you are interested in buying a property. Rents are always subject to negotiation: important points in bargaining are:

(a) the fact that respectable expats are generally considered desirable tenants,
(b) length of stay (leases are usually for one year and include a refundable deposit),
(c) your company and status (strangely enough, if you are important and rich you might get a cheaper rent), and
(d) the location of the house.

Unless you are moving into a company house, the chances are you will be employing the services of housing agents. These advertise daily in the English language newspapers and most are well established. Any one of them will, without charge, pick you up at your convenience and show you houses within the area and price range you have in mind. Don't be surprised if other areas are suggested and don't necessarily dismiss them in favour of Sukhumvit, where most foreigners live. Feel no compunction about utilising the services of as many agents as you have time for and don't be surprised to be shown the same house by different agents quoting different prices. Be aware that the agent gets a commission (two weeks' rent) from the landlord, not the tenant: he has an interest to rent high but also to rent fast. Agents are friendly but they are in the game for the money. If they admit that the house 'occasionally floods just a little bit,' it probably means the house is under water several weeks a year. Steer clear of anywhere near construction works. In Thailand building work can continue 24 hours a day, seven days a week.

When you have decided what you want, be prepared to bargain with an air of detachment. Some house-hunters are unscrupulous enough to offer a present to the agent on condition he will drive down the price with the landlord. Having been introduced to the landlord, it is not a good idea to try to deal direct and cut out the agent; a good landlord would not do it.

Outside Bangkok, rents are very much cheaper. Indeed, they can be ridiculously cheap if you are really upcountry. Bargain just the same and check out what is included.

Of course, if the company is paying the rent, be aware that there are some really beautiful modern or traditional houses on the market at very high prices.

However much you have to pay, it should not take long to find accommodation. No need to jump at the first thing. Many landlords are excellent, some less so. Make sure all repairs and agreed changes are completed before you move in or sign the contract, at which point you pay the deposit, which is usually three months' rent.

Bathrooms

Western-style sit-down toilets and toilet-paper are to be found in all posh offices and hotels and in almost all houses or flats rented to expats. They are a fairly recent innovation. If you find footprints on the toilet seat, it is because some Thais have not yet perfected the habit of sitting down on the job. For them, the sit-down flush toilet is as much an item of culture shock as the squat toilet is for you. It should be obvious, but it isn't, so here are the very basic do's and don'ts of relieving yourself in most Thai toilets.

1. Squat, or come as close as you can to squatting, with the backside over the hole, not on it (do not sit or stand).
2. Males should bear in mind that trousers pulled down a distance sufficient for a sit-down toilet will leave your pockets pointed straight down the hole of a squat toilet. Retrieval of coins, comb and wallet could be unpleasant.
3. If paper is provided, it is usually placed in a basket after use, not dropped down the hole. This practice is not, as some foreigners think, to allow recycling but to prevent the drainage system blocking up.
4. If there is no paper, there is usually a jar of water and a scoop. The water is used to clean your backside. Human beings have been doing this for centuries.

Apart from the basic hole, a jar of water and one nail to hold your clothes, traditional Thai bathrooms are spartan. If you need to bathe under these conditions, scoop the water from the jar and throw it over your naked body. You will soon get to like this method of bathing. It is certainly a lot surer than the average 'modern' Bangkok shower that dribbles at best and stops just as you get soaped up.

If you are really upcountry, you will often find no bathroom at all, just a well, stream or river. In these circumstances most people bathe only at dawn and dusk, which means you will have lots of company. For once, do as they do.

In recent years the West has woken up to the merits of a clean backside and a Swiss toilet might now contain both wet and dry paper. The Thais have gone one better and combined tradition with modern convenience: the latest toilets come equipped with a water-gun hose. Once try, always use!

Boats

Although Bangkok's *khlongs* (canals) are disappearing fast, an elaborate network of waterways continues to connect up many parts of the city. With a bit of planning, many of the worst traffic jams can be avoided by taking to the boats. River buses go up and down the Chao Phya River with amazing reliability and regularity. There are some twenty main stops. Useful ones for you to know are (from upriver, north, to downriver, south):

- *Tha Theves* and *Tha Wisut Kasat*, a short taxi or bus ride on uncrowded streets to ESCAP and Thai government offices.
- *Tha Maharat* and *Tha Chang*, you can walk to Thammasat and Silapakorn Universities, Sanam Luang (Phramane), National Theatre and National Museum.
- *Tha Ratchawong*, for Chinatown.
- *Tha Wat Muang Kai* and *Tha Orien*, for the main Post Office on New Road, French Embassy, Oriental Hotel, and ends of Silom Road and Surawong Road.
- *Tha Sathorn Tai*, for Sathorn Road.

River bus fares are cheap and fixed but vary according to the number of stops, so you need to be able to tell the conductor where you are going. Try them. Apart from considerations of convenience, they open up a new world. A great way to start the day.

There are other river buses on canals throughout the city. Particularly useful is the route along the New Petburi side of Sukhumvit that passes Phratu Nam and goes right across the city. Check the fare and destination before climbing aboard.

Buses

Thai buses have a character and culture of their own. The festoons of flower garlands swinging in front of the driver's face, the ritual of the ticket clipping and the bus race are all a daily part of Bangkok culture.

Visitors should be aware that drivers and money collectors work largely on a commission basis. This explains why they are happy to pack as many people as possible into the bus, scramble around inside and outside collecting fares, and try to beat the competition to the next stop.

On buses, the word *pai* means 'go' and the word *pai* means 'stop'. Confusing for the visitor, but, because of tone and vowel-length distinctions, two completely different words to a Thai.

Buses go everywhere. You stick your hand out to stop one if you are waiting for it and signal the conductor if you are on it. Ordinary buses (the ones with people hanging out of the doorways) are very, very cheap. Air-conditioned buses are just cheap. There is a basic fare which doubles for really long distances.

Hang on tight. Watch your back pockets and handbags. And remember, monks sit on the back seat.

Clothing

Bangkok is hot and humid all year long, so light-weight clothing within the limits of propriety is a must. It is often difficult or impossible to find large sizes, but almost anything, including shoes, can be made to measure at very reasonable prices.

Many of the big-footed prefer to bring in a good supply of footwear. And don't forget the pullovers, required in the north during the beautiful winter months and very often just as necessary in Bangkok's over-air-conditioned offices and theatres.

Driving

If you intend to drive in Thailand, be aware that the norms of courtesy and deference described in this book do not apply on the road. Instead, hierarchical rules of power are transferred to the vehicles themselves; might is right. At the top of the hierarchy are ten-wheel trucks, army tanks, bulldozers, steamrollers and six-wheel trucks that drive around dropping stones and mud onto the roads. In the middle come buses, in their many forms. And at the bottom are cars, motorcycles, bicycles and other motor and man-powered vehicles. The death rate on the roads is extremely high.

Accidents can be settled on the spot by an agreed exchange of money. Serious accidents involve the authorities but if everyone agrees and no serious laws have been broken even fatalities can be settled by compensation. This is more the norm the more upcountry you go. Be aware that the car driver who puts a cyclist in hospital will normally be expected to pay the medical bills regardless of blame. Comprehensive insurance is a good idea.

You will be confused by the fact that buses, quite legally, often travel in the opposite direction to everybody else on one-way streets. International signs exist (not always in places where they can be seen), but many signs are only written in Thai. Ignorance of the law, or the plea that you do not read Thai is, of course, no excuse whatsoever.

International driving licences are recognised. If you don't have one, you can pass your test without moving out of the car park. If you have a licence from another country, you may obtain a Thai one by taking a supply of photographs (passport-size) and as many one hundred baht notes to Police Registration Division, Phaholyothin Road.

Driving is on the left, most of the time.

Electricity
240 volts AC, with fluctuations in power and, depending on where you stay, occasional blackouts. Nothing is earthed and everything has two pin plugs.

Health

Take things easy for the first few weeks in your new environment; the climate and the sensory effects of culture shock will make you feel tired. Don't try to change your food and drink habits overnight, or you will get sick.

Most foreigners live in fear of hepatitis, malaria and cholera. Dangers are exaggerated in travellers' tales, but if you are the worrying kind or will be spending time in remote areas, immunising injections and tablets exist. Anti-tetanus jabs are also worth having.

If you are bitten by a dog, go straight to a reliable doctor. Rabid dogs do not always froth at the mouth. 'Worms' are contracted by going barefoot; wear shoes outside the house. Mosquitoes can be kept at bay by lighting mosquito coils, which burn slowly throughout the night, or by plugging in one of several forms of electric killer. Boil water for at least five minutes or buy it in bottles. Like cooking gas, drinking water can be delivered to your house by the large bottle or in crated smaller bottles that fit in the fridge. There are many excellent doctors and dentists in Bangkok, most of whom speak English. Upcountry, good health services are not so easy to find.

Hospitals

New super hospitals are going up every day. Prices are low, treatment generally good and rooms luxurious. Listed below are a few that have stood the test of a generation or two of expats. All would put the average UK hospital to shame.

University Teaching Hospitals:
- Chulalongkorn, corner of Rama IV and Rajdamri Road, Tel: 2528131
- Ramathibodi, Rama VI Road, Tel: 2813566
- Siriraj, Thonburi, Tel: 4110241

Private:
- Bangkok Adventist Hospital, 430 Pitsanuloke Road, Tel: 2811422/ 2821100

- Bangkok Christian Hospital, 124 Silom Road, Tel: 2336981
- Bangkok Nursing Home, Convent Road, Tel: 2332610-9 (24-hour ambulance service)
- Payathai 1 Hospital, Sri Ayudhya Road
- Payathai 2 Hospital, Paholyothin Road
- Prommitr Hospital, 12 Soi Prommitr Sukhumvit, Tel: 3921095
- Saint Louis Hospital, 215 Sathorn Tai, Tel: 2112769
- Samitivej Hospital, Soi 49, Sukhumvit Road

LIBRARIES

- AUA, 179 Rajdamri Road, Tel. 2524021
- British Council, 428 Soi 2 Siam Square, Rama I Road, Tel. 2526136
- Neilson Hays, 195 Suriwongse Road, Tel. 2331731
- Siam Society, 131 Soi Asoke, Sukhumvit, Tel. 3914401
- Thailand Information Centre, Chulalongkorn University (Henri Dunant side, opposite Dept. of Political Sciences)

Police

Usually respond slowly to emergency calls. Visitors may call the following number between 8 a.m. and midnight and they should get a reply in English: 2815051 or 2810372. Try not to have an emergency after midnight.

The best thing to do, however, is locate your nearest police station and get its number(s). Very few policemen can speak anything but Thai.

Railways

There is a train service within Bangkok which is practically unused by visitors. Stations are hidden away and trains are infrequent but they do leave on time and, if slow by international standards, are very fast in comparison to inner-city road transport. It is also easier for the visitor to know when to get off (station signs are written in English). Trains run from the central train station (where timetables are available) located right in town. One line goes out to Don Muang airport, and a second goes through Makkasan, follows New Phetburi and passes King Mongkut Institute of Technology before going all the way to Aranyapratet on the Cambodian border.

Travelling long distances by train can be pleasant if you have the time and if you travel first- or second-class. Sleeping berths, food, drinks and service (both official and unofficial) must rank among the best in the world. Only one problem about long-distance trains: they are slow, very slow or unbelievably slow. Or, as the Thai timetables put it, Express, Rapid and Normal.

Schools

It is not really legal for foreign children to attend Thai schools but nobody minds. Few do so because of the language problem. If you are living outside of Bangkok or Chiengmai and want to keep the family together, there is no choice other than a local school. Even in relatively small district towns, there are usually fee-paying and non-fee-paying schools. Fees, for most foreigners, are too small to worry about, but they provide that little extra resource which allows a school to attract better teachers and keep the school in reasonable repair. Classes in both school types are large, 30–40 pupils on average, and there is therefore little personal attention. Rote learning methods prevail (not necessarily a bad thing for a foreigner since it assists passive language learning by constant repetition).

The younger your child, the more we would recommend you consider a Thai school. Standards in some of Bangkok's Thai nursery schools are very good; your under-seven child could play and learn (including Thai and English) alongside the children of the rich and powerful in pleasant surroundings which often include playground and swimming pool. Optional facilities are usually available for Thai dancing and music classes.

If your child has been to a Thai nursery school he or she might be able to cope with a Thai primary school. Grade One is for 6–7-year-olds and starts from scratch. The curriculum is national and the language of instruction is Thai (central dialect). There is a good element of language learning during the first year at school: it starts with learning the Thai alphabet by heart. English is also taught from the first year and, for the English-speaking child, it can provide a psychological boost and increases the child's status. (Foreign children should try not to correct the teacher's English!)

Foreign children at Thai schools must conform. Every morning children line up and pay respect to the Thai flag. Things are done very much by the rule book and by the bell. Not much hint so far of Montessori methods. Uniforms are worn, perhaps with changes on certain days of the week. Days are long, usually 8 a.m. to 3:30 p.m.

If your child is much over seven and has no prior knowledge of Thai, it would be difficult or impossible to fit him into a Thai school. There is then only the choice of the (US curriculum) International School in Bangkok and Bangkok Patana School (UK curriculum), which teach in English. There are also three International Schools in Chiengmai of which Lana International School of Thailand (LIST) is gaining a good reputation. There are also small international schools in Phuket and Pattaya. There is a cramped French language school, which accepts non-French nationals, at the Alliance Française on Sathorn Tai Road. The two largest English medium schools are on the outskirts of Bangkok, making long bus journeys for the children. School days are much shorter than Thai schools and fees are so high that many foreigners cannot meet them unless the company pays. Very steep entrance fees discourage enrolment if children plan to be in the country for only six months to one year.

If both Thai medium and English medium schools are not appropriate and you want your child (children) with you in Thailand, and the period away from school is a year or less, you might consider teaching the child yourself. Assistance will be needed and preparation is essential.

If the child is to return to the same school after the Thailand experience, he will have the incentive of wanting to move up with his cohort. The child should correspond regularly with his class back home, where a sensible teacher will use his letters and photographs as a teaching resource. Obtain before leaving all set books for the year and a general framework which will allow you to set targets. Correspondence courses exist in most subjects at most secondary levels.

Don't get bogged down in worry that your child is not keeping up with the children back home. Remember you are in Thailand. One year is enough for a child, and his mother, to learn basic Thai, so language instruction can be included along with Thai history and culture. Space achieved targets in auto-education with trips around Thailand, which in themselves are quite an education and something to write home about.

Servants

Beware of agencies offering cheap servants. Recommendations from Thais at the office or the neighbours or the landlord are most likely to obtain you somebody you can trust, but who speaks no English. For a maid who speaks a few words of English badly, expect to pay about three times what a Thai would normally pay his servant. Be aware that there are labour laws in Thailand (even if your servant is unaware) and console yourself with the fact that you are probably paying not much more than the minimum legal wage.

To an extent, the wage differential is justified. The foreigner often does not provide accommodation or food and expects one servant to do everything. There are no other servants to talk to, laugh with and form the social group which makes work bearable and sometimes fun. Working for foreigners can be a lonely business; it can also be confusing getting used to their strange ways and it is inevitably temporary—two or three years at the most then it will be goodbye. Some servants really become attached to their families, particularly the children, and you might well become equally attached to your servant and treat her well. But you will one day be gone.

Finding a servant is not difficult, but no longer are there queues at the gate. Indeed many young people prefer to enter the new opportunities offered by industry and commerce. If you do not inherit house and servant/s from your predecessor and require an English speaker of sorts, you can go along on Monday morning to an American Women's Club in the AUA compound (next to the 'thrift shop') on Rajdamri Road. For a small fee you can meet and talk to an assembly of left-behind maids looking for a job. Most have references. Find somebody of a pleasant nature rather than somebody who looks like they can clearly do the work. You should clarify:

1. Salary,
2. Working hours,
3. Work to be done,
4. Days off,
5. If accommodation and food are included.

Make up your mind beforehand your position on all of these points and do not bargain. A maid who is prepared to question you on any of them is quite likely to end up in a conflict situation in your home. And this is the last thing either of you want.

In addition to salary (usually paid monthly, but many maids prefer a small weekly advance), it is usual to give small gifts (which should certainly include money) at New Year, Thai New Year and birthdays. As a rough guide count on giving over one year an amount somewhat over one month's salary. One day off a week is usual and in addition days off for Thai religious holidays (but not all national holidays) and, within limits, family occasions (weddings and funerals). Some small financial help would be normal if the servant is sick. No fixed annual holiday (they take off while you are away), but just about all servants who originate from the North or Northeast will expect to return home for Thai New Year (13–15 April). On separation one month's salary for each year of service is normal.

Signs

Some road signs, such as BEWARE OF THE PEDESTRIANS and the equally enigmatic BETTER LATE THAN NEVER are, for whatever reason, translated into English. Most of the others, unimportant things like STOP and DANGER, are usually written only in Thai. Signs written only in Thai, tacked onto a traffic light, may look very much alike to the non-Thai reader. 'Turn left whenever you like' means you can ignore the red light and turn left: if in the left lane. 'Turn left only when the lights change' means something very different. Even if you can slowly decipher a bit of Thai, you are not likely to get much beyond 'Turn left ...' if it is the first of these two signs, before honking horns from behind help you guess which one it is.

Road names are written in Thai with a very small English transliteration underneath. If you can read it at all, be prepared for some surprises. Transliteration sometimes represents the sound and at other times is a literal transliteration of all the Thai letters, which in Thai carry different pronunciations, depending on their place in a syllable, and in a number of cases are not pronounced at all.

Things are made no easier for the visitor by the fact that some names are translated instead of transliterated. Thus, *Thanon Vitayu* becomes Wireless Road on the English part of the sign. A few people might understand it if the visitor looking for this popular street (which hosts such important institutions as Lumpini Police Station and the American, Spanish and a few other embassies) said, or tried to say, 'Vitayu'; very few would understand 'Wireless Road'.

In an inscrutable exercise in mystic nomenclature, some places have been given an English name which is neither a translation nor a transliteration. *Charoen Krung*, literally 'prosperous city', and probably one of the oldest roads in town, bears the English name 'New Road'.

Taxis

Nowhere is change more evident than in the taxi driver's world. After decades of failed attempts to get drivers to wear hats, laws suddenly coincided with consumer needs and the 1990s saw a rapid transition to air-conditioned taxis with meters that work.

Taking a taxi used to be an artform and a sure way to distinguish a Thailand-hand from a new-arrival. Now only *tuk-tuks* and motorcycle-taxis require the ritual of bargaining. To get a taxi, you now just wave your hand and get in as you would in New York. Well, almost. You will still find drivers who don't want to go where you are going. This might be because it is near the end of their taxi-hire shift and they have to get the vehicle back to base or pay extra. Or it might be because the driver feels like a bowl of noodles with his friends and you are not going in his direction. Or it might be because your destination is too near and he is in a location where he might pick up a better fare.

If the last reason applies, he will probably tell you (in Thai). This is an appropriate time to hop into a *tuk-tuk*, which usually run shorter journeys within a home territory. The fare for the journey must be agreed in advance, as you hang hesitantly one hand and one foot on the framework. In most locations and at most times the sheer number of empty vehicles means you are in a buyer's market. Thus, if the price quoted for a journey seems too high and you cannot clinch a satisfactory deal within four seconds, step aside and stop the next one. The problem for the visitor is not getting a *tuk-tuk* or paying the price but knowing where he is going and how much the fare should be.

Armed with this knowledge, the passenger has the advantage at the opening of negotiations. The longer bargaining continues, the more advantage passes to the driver. This is because, although most *tuk-tuk* drivers demonstrate computer-like powers of calculation, some thinking time is required. You name the destination. Immediately, the computer-brain calculates distance, traffic and weather conditions and any special roadworks on the way and evaluates the passenger (by firmness and clarity of the destination statement). This is all accomplished in the two seconds it takes to turn the head woefully in the direction of the proposed destination to indicate that traffic conditions are so bad and the goal so far away that the price of petrol will have gone up before you arrive. Then out pops a price.

The first price is always too high. You can short-circuit the driver's thought-process by a slightly haughty 'ha' or 'ho' and state the exact price or 5 baht below in take-it-or-leave-it terms. A nod of the head indicates acceptance. A cloud of exhaust fumes in your face indicates you should pitch a little higher with the next *tuk-tuk* or take the bus.

Motorcycle taxis have mushroomed as a 1990s service industry because of the clogged streets (a problem which the armadas of taxis and *tuk-tuks* do nothing to alleviate). There are two types. One just runs up and down a long *soi* for a fixed price of a few baht. The other will take you anywhere at an agreed (bargained) fare. Introduction of laws making crash helmets compulsory hit the trade for a while, but now many lady-commuters carry a cloth to put between hair and the helmet supplied by the motor-cyclist. Many a businessman who thought he would never be seen dead on a motorbike learns to appreciate this service. Hopelessly stuck in a traffic jam, the possibility always exists to get out of a taxi or chauffeur-driven car and hop onto a humble speed machine in order to make that important meeting.

Tipping, in whatever type of taxi, is not usual. In those in which you bargain for your fare, it is illogical. But don't worry too much about logic when travelling in Thailand.

Thai Language Classes

The Thai language is very beautiful but very difficult for westerners, few of whom have the time to learn anything more than basics. Even the basics take a lot of time and effort. Lots of small language schools and private tutors are to be found in Bangkok. Complete beginners could not do better than to enrol at the AUA, 179 Rajdamri Road, Tel. 2527067, which takes in a fresh batch of students (intensive or evening) every five weeks and has a choice of modern language learning methods to suit your mind and requirements.

CULTURAL QUIZ

To function positively and effectively in a new culture requires much more than simply learning a list of social taboos. To be successful, you must get a 'feel' for situations so that 'correct' behaviour comes almost naturally. This, of course, is something that can come only with time and experience, after plenty of mistakes and much frustration. To get you thinking in terms of social situations rather than rules of 'what not to do', this chapter is devoted to a Thai culture quiz. Situations 1–9 are likely to be met by any visitor; situations 10–18 are geared towards the expat manager.

Human beings being what they are, there is no absolutely correct response to any particular situation. Judgement of 'right' and 'wrong' is therefore bound to be somewhat arbitrary and subjective. Culture is learnt but it is by no means static enough to quantify, except for fun.

Answers are graded on a scale of 10, from –5 to + 5 (with the occasional –10 for real bloomers). Neutral responses are given zero. The childish use of plus and minus signs is to emphasise that whatever your response, it has positive or negative influences on the development of a situation.

There are several ways of tackling the quiz. The simplest way is to follow the instructions ('choose one', 'select as appropriate', etc.), note the response you think correct and check the score given. Score zero and you are safe; a minus score and you should read this book again before you are completely floored by culture shock.

If you don't feel like doing a quiz, simply read through the situations and comments. Even if you disagree with what we say you will be thinking situationally. If you are two or more, or a classroom, compare your views—it's more fun.

If you want to do the test 'fairly', cover the score column and 'Comments', where the answers and rationale for the answers are written.

Use a pencil to permit somebody else to do the quiz.

Don't take the marks too seriously; we didn't.

SITUATION ONE

Having paid the bill in a restaurant, the waitress brings your change on a tray. You pick it up, leaving behind a tip. She smiles beautifully and *wais* you before picking up the money. Do you: (choose one)

    A Ignore her.
    B Put another 5 baht on the tray.
    C Smile and carry on talking to your friends.
    D Stand up and return the *wai*.
    E Raise your hands casually in a low *wai* while remaining seated.

Comments

Only *A* and *C* are normal. *E* would be odd and *D* could be interpreted as sarcasm and, therefore, rudeness. To do *B* would certainly invoke a further beautiful smile and *wai*. It would, of course, bring you back to the beginning but might be worth the money if the waitress is genuinely amused. We have given this response a minus because there is a suggestion of playing with people purely for your own amusement. If your friends laugh, the waitress could be embarrassed.

Score

A   0

B –1

C +5

D –5

E –3

SITUATION TWO

You call on a Thai friend to invite him out to eat. He accepts and you are just about to get into the car when his Thai friends draw up. They explain to him that they are going to Nick's Restaurant and ask him to join them. Your friend says 'meet you there'. As you drive off, wondering how much your friend's largess will cost you and what kind of a boring time you are in for with everybody speaking Thai except for you, your friend says, 'Where shall we eat, how about the Sorn Daeng?' Do you reply: (choose one)

   A   Of course not, you just told your friends we would be at Nick's.

   B   O.K. Let's go there.

   C   Good idea, we can always drop by Nick's later on.

   D   Yes, I'd like to go there. But won't your friends be waiting for us at Nick's?

   E   If you don't want to meet your friends, why didn't you just say we were going to dinner somewhere else and leave it at that?

Comments

An *E* type reply would be very bad manners, however good a friend he is. It betrays a stark western reasoning; by all means think it, but don't say it. The accusing tone is quite unjustified since your friend was simply trying to be polite to everybody. For him to tell the others that the two of you were going to dinner without inviting them along would suggest that both of you had no time for them; since eating together is a mark of friendship, this suggestion could be interpreted as a repudiation of their friendship. *To invite someone to eat with you is a very basic part of Thai personality.* It is also a speech habit and the words are therefore not as literally meaningful as the translation would be in the west.

Choice *D* sounds reasonable but contains an element of criticism. It also places your friend in a difficult position, making him choose between your wishes and meeting his friends. Choice *A* is out because it directly criticises your friend. Choice *B* is fine, assuming you really don't want to be with his friends. Choice *C* is best, since you reaffirm your friend's invitation to his friends. (You do not, of course, remember to drop by unless you want to.) If you do walk into the Sorn Daeng and find your friend's friends there, you smile and join them for dinner!

Score

A –3

B +4

C +5

D –2

E –5

SITUATION THREE

While visiting the grounds of a *Wat*, a group of friendly people sitting in the *sala* invite you to sit down with them and eat hot curry and drink rice wine. You dislike both and have no wish to join the group. Do you: (one response)

    A Lie and say you have just eaten.

    B Say you are sorry but you don't have time.

    C Refuse, explaining that you cannot take curry and rice wine.

    D Eat a little bit, hoping to get away quickly.

    E Ignore them and hurry away.

Comments

In Thai, invitations to eat are as frequent and as sincere as inquiries after the state of one's health in English. 'Eaten already' *(A)* is the standard polite response. Not having time for something or for somebody *(B)* is no excuse at all in Thailand; this response implies a mild indirect insult to the inviters. Choice *C* is sensible, but your would-be hosts are likely to find other things that they think you would like. Choice *D* is polite but unnecessary; it is also very difficult to leave quickly and gracefully after eating a little. Ignoring them *(E)* is not likely to bother the group very much, but if you hurry away from every situation like this one, you will not benefit at all from your stay in Thailand.

If you do wish to join the group, it is polite, but not essential, to excuse yourself and wait for the invitation to be repeated; at which point, sit down and tuck in.

In more formal situations (if you are attending a family ceremony, for example), the 'eaten already' excuse is not acceptable and to refuse to eat for any reason would be bad manners.

Score

A +5

B −1

C 0

D 0

E −2

SITUATION FOUR

You stop a young Thai man in the street and ask him the way. He points in the direction he is walking and offers to show you. As you are walking and talking, he takes your hand. Do you:

  A Pull your hand away and walk off by yourself.
  B Grin and bear it.
  C Explain that you are not used to this kind of thing and gently withdraw your hand.
  D Grin and enjoy it.
  E Ruffle his hair with your free hand.

Comments

Taking the hand of complete strangers is not standard behaviour in Thailand, but if you are a man be prepared for it to happen more often than back home. The action does not in itself imply homosexuality.

Man answering:

If you do enjoy it, choice *D* is right for you. If you do not enjoy it, or if you are worried about what your *farang* friends will say if they see you, there is no need to put up with it (*B*). Taking the *C* path while maintaining a friendly manner will save everybody embarrassment; for once explanations, or attempted explanations, are in order. A safe and inoffensive alternative is to occupy your nearside hand by carrying something in it.

Woman answering:

The stranger is being rude to you. Hesitancy will encourage his advances. Time for action. Even if you do enjoy holding hands with strangers (or friends) of the opposite sex, the street is not the place for it!

Either sex:

Ruffle hair and you are, of course, asking for all the trouble you might get.

	Man	Woman
A	−5	+5
B	0	−5
C	+4	−1
D	+5	−5
E	−10	10

SITUATION FIVE

Choose the most appropriate way of saying 'thank you' in each of the following situations from the following responses: (One choice for each.)

(i) no reaction; (ii) smile; (iii) smile and nod;
(iv) 'thank you'; (v) wai

- A A taxi driver gives you change after you pay the fare.
- B A monk gives you something.
- C A hotel boy opens the door for you.
- D You buy something from a street vendor who says 'thank you' to you.
- E Your maid informs you that she has just killed a poisonous snake about to bite your son.
- F A stranger points out the location of a shop you are looking for.
- G A polite immigration officer extends your visa to stay in Thailand without making you come back the next day.

	no reaction	smile	smile & nod	'thank you'	wai
A	+5	+5	0	−1	−5
B	−5	−2	−1	0	+5
C	+4	+5	−1	−5	−10
D	0	+5	+4	−1	−5
E	−10	−5	−1	+5	+2
F	−5	+2	+4	+5	−3
G	−10	−2	−1	+5	+2

Comments

This exercise should show that the form gratitude expression takes in Thailand depends partly on the service performed (as it does in the west), but much more on the status of the doer. Other factors, not included here, are age and likeability. For the same service, the elderly are thanked somewhat more than the young. If you like a particular taxi driver and he has performed well, a verbal 'thank you' is not out of place.

SITUATION SIX

You are sitting with a Thai friend and his 7-year-old child on a crowded bus, when an old man enters. Would you: (one choice)

A Do nothing.
B Ask the child to give up his seat to allow the old man to sit.
C Ask your friend to put his child on his lap to make room for the old man.
D Give up your seat for the old man.
E Give the old man your seat and pay his fare.

Comments

You give up your seat for the old man (choice D) because of respect for his age. Since children are valued more than anything else, they are given the comparative safety of a seat on the bus and not expected to stand for their elders. Choice B is therefore out. If your friend spontaneously puts his child on his lap, that's fine. But suggesting he do so (choice C) implies criticism. Doing nothing (choice A) is, in today's world, not too bad. Paying the old man's fare, unless he asks you, is insulting. If he does ask you, don't give up your seat.

Score

A 0	D +5
B –5	E –2
C –2	

SITUATION SEVEN

You are wandering along, minding your own business, when a stranger sitting at a stall by the roadside says 'You!' at you. Do you: (one response)

- *A* Assume he is looking for trouble and hurry on by.
- *B* Say 'You!' in return.
- *C* Carry on walking.
- *D* Tell him that it is rude to say 'You!'
- *E* Point your foot at him.

Comments

'You!', 'Hey, you!' or 'Mister!' could be the first English words you hear spoken by a Thai—small words that leave a bad impression on thousands of foreign visitors every year. However tolerant you are, 'You!' is almost certain to annoy. However, pointing a foot at the offender (*E*) is about as appropriate as giving a *wai*, and likely to get you into lots of well-deserved trouble. Choice *A* is playing it safe, but it is wrong to assume the caller is looking for trouble. Unless you can say it in Thai, telling him it is rude to say 'You!' (*D*) will not get you far, since Thais who say 'You!' rarely speak more than six words of English (all of them annoying); you will also have got yourself into a rather negative situation instead of neutralising an annoying one. Choice *B*, saying 'You!' in return is not likely to get you into trouble, but it is likely to reinforce the unfortunate behaviour pattern.

If you want to attract somebody's attention, it is acceptable to say the Thai equivalents of 'You', 'Mister' or 'Lady'. Thais do it. But they inevitably pick a polite word for 'You' and add the respect suffix. And, most importantly, they have some reason for attracting attention (just to see the *farang* turn round is not a good reason). So, although the caller is unlikely to wish to be rude, this is really a time for the neutral response. Give a flimsy smile if you like, but walk on by. Don't let an inappropriate response to such a tiny thing spoil one second of your stay in Thailand. Remember, 99 per cent of Thais would never dream of saying 'Hey, you!' and most of the 1 per cent would rather say 'Excuse me, Sir,' if only they knew the words.

Score

A 0

B –4

C +5

D –1

E –5

SITUATION EIGHT

When assessing your relative status, a Thai is likely to consider which of the following points? (Select as many as you think appropriate.)

    A   Social connections

    B   Family

    C   Education

    D   Wage/wealth

    E   Occupation

    F   Dress and manners

    G   Age

    H   Car and house

    I   Religion

    J   Race

    K   Ability to speak Thai

    L   Friendliness

Comments

Almost everything is a pointer to your status, particularly the first five points on this list. However, religion, race, linguistic ability and friendliness play no part. Flattery about fair skin or exaggerated compliments on your ability to say a few words in Thai should not be confused with status.

	Selected	Not Selected
A	+1	–2
B	+1	–2
C	+1	–2
D	+1	–2
E	+1	–2
F	+1	–2
G	+1	–2
H	+1	–2
I	–5	+1
J	–5	+1
K	–5	+1
L	–5	+1

DID WE REALLY HAVE TO GET DRESSED UP?

SITUATION NINE

A foreigner who wants to make himself popular with Thais should follow which of the following maxims? (Select as many as you think appropriate.)

- A   Never do or say anything to cause offence.
- B   Be honest and say exactly what you think.
- C   Be yourself and people will respect you for it.
- D   Be generous.
- E   Do as the Thais do.
- F   Smile and take it easy.

Comments

In any particular situation, the amount of damage done by 'saying what you think' (*B*) and 'being yourself' (*C*) would depend on what you think and what you are.

As a guiding principle covering all situations, it is much safer to avoid making a bad impression (*A*) than to pursue popularity. The foreigner who really craves popularity can buy it (*D*), although generosity without politeness will not achieve very much.

Doing 'as the Thais do' (*E*) is the most dangerous advice without the rider 'as Thais of equal status do'. You do not sit cross-legged in front of a monk, although he is sitting this way. You do not return the same *wai* you receive, etc.

If really in doubt about what to do, do nothing, just smile and take it easy; this is the safest and surest way to popularity.

Score

A +5

B –5

C –5

D +5

E –5

F +5

SITUATION TEN

You are working in Thailand. You visit a project site where the work is a year behind schedule. During a tour of the site you find no good reason for the delays. After the visit, you are invited to give your impressions to the Thai manager and staff of the project. Do you: (choose one)

A Tell them the rate of progress is appalling and if they don't pull up their socks, they will all be sacked.

B Ask them collectively the reason for the delays.

C Single out the project manager and ask him to account for the slow progress.

D Go through the aims and history of the project, pointing out all difficulties, however minor, and praising the team for over-coming these difficulties to the extent that work can now proceed as originally planned.

E Make an unfavourable comparison with progress on a similar project and give a mild pep talk.

Comments

The rule here, as everywhere, is to avoid criticism. If your words are to have any positive impact, you must be respected and liked. Respect is granted automatically because of your status, but make yourself unpopular and you are unlikely to get very far. The D approach is ideal for situations like this, where you have as long as you like to talk to a captive audience without interruption. Be careful that praise for very minor achievements does not lapse into the kind of sarcasm which could draw a relaxing laugh in the west but would fuel the tension in Thailand. The real advantages of the D technique is that it gains you popularity with the entire workforce, makes it clear that whatever happened in the past was nobody's fault and need not affect the future and leaves you in a good position to work closely with the project manager. When alone with him, and if you are sure he likes you, you might consider mentioning that the really big bosses are making things difficult for you by always asking for reports on this project (the 'they don't understand the difficulties' approach). Singling out an individual for public criticism (*C*) would certainly not improve his performance and is likely to cause further delays in project implementation. Similarly, collective criticism, whether direct (*A*) or indirect (*E*), will have the opposite effect to that intended.

Asking the reason for delays (*B*), even in a 'let's tackle this problem together' spirit, is most likely to draw an embarrassing silence that is difficult to follow; the silence may be due to reluctance to speak out in public; it could, however, be interpreted as implying that no good reason exists for the delays.

The fact that you found no reason for delays during a brief guided tour for big shots does not mean no reason exists. If people like you and find you sympathetic, they will find ways of letting you know if the foreman is pocketing 20 per cent of the workmen's wages.

Score

A –5

B   0

C –10

D +5

E –1

SITUATION TWELVE

You receive a printed invitation to an administration clerk's wedding to take place early Saturday morning. You want to maintain good relations, but this is the third wedding in four months; you do not know her family or the groom and you would much rather stay at home, get up late and play with the kids. Do you:

A   Make the effort to go in order to maintain good relations.

B   Thank her for the invitation and simply not turn up.

C   Drop by for a short period and leave.

229

    D Give her an envelope with a sizeable amount of money inside
       and say you are sorry you cannot make it.
    E Give the envelope to a colleague who is certain to attend.

Comments

Any occasion with printed invitations, particularly weddings, cannot
simply be ignored (*B*) in the same way that a casual verbal invitation
could be. Putting yourself, and your family, out in order to attend (*A*
and *C*) is not necessary. It is, however, necessary to give money and
not a miserly amount. This can either be given to your clerk (*D*) or to
a colleague (*E*) who will put it on the special tray provided. Your
envelope should, of course, be clearly marked with your name so that
your generosity is credited (and excellent relations maintained).

Score

A 0

B –5

C 0

D +5

E +5

SITUATION THIRTEEN

A young staff member never speaks to you and seems to have avoided
you ever since you arrived. When she/he has work to give you, it is
usually passed through another person. Her/his work seems all right.
At first you thought he/she was simply shy. But you see him/her
happily chatting with other staff members and even outsiders. You
begin to feel that unwittingly you might have offended the staff
member. Do you:

    A Call the person into your office for a coffee and a chat and
       discreetly ask if everything is all right.
    B Ask your secretary to find out what the problem is.

C Encourage more interaction by giving the person duties that require more contact.

D Make a point of speaking socially to the person whenever you pass her/him.

E Let things continue as they are.

Comments

It is perfectly normal and proper in a Thai work setting for an inferior to maintain social distance from the boss. Individuals vary, but some degree of *krengjai* feeling should be there if you are getting due respect. This does not mean that your staff should be afraid to talk to you; with some you might get more talk than you want and with others, like this staff member, hardly any communication at all. Deliberately trying to make the individual 'open up' (A) is likely to leave your staff member confused and wondering if he/she has done something wrong (or if you are making sexual advances). B will definitely suggest that you are not satisfied (and that therefore the staff member is at fault). C or D, while not too bad, would mean singling out the staff member. If you have the time and inclination to speak a few words to staff members when you pass each of them, try not to ignore this one because of seeming lack of response: i.e., treat him/her as you would anybody else. Let things continue. You probably have not offended—the person was always reserved (if a normally chatty person suddenly clams up, however, do begin to wonder if there is some reason that could include you). While Thais are becoming increasingly used to working with *farang* and many adjust their behaviour accordingly, some cannot. Please don't push them to do so.

Score

A –5

B –5

C –1

D –1

E +5

SITUATION FOURTEEN

One of your office staff asks to see you and informs you that a driver is stealing office supplies regularly. You ask how he knows and he claims to have witnessed, along with other staff members, at least one theft. However, he explains that the driver has a reputation as a tough guy and that everybody is afraid to confront him. He also asks you not to involve him in your investigations. Do you:

A   Sack the driver.
B   Insist that the informant confront the accused in your presence and if he refuses ignore the matter.
C   Call in the police.
D   See all your staff one by one and ask them if they have seen anything.
E   See all staff together, including the driver, for a showdown.

Comments

This is serious. You must come to a quick decision which your staff will accept as fair. You cannot sack one man only on the word of another (*A*). Thieves are often tough guys and it is sensible to a Thai to avoid any possibility of personal reprisal, so don't blame staff for not wanting to point a finger at the accused. Seeing everybody together (*E*) could be taken as a sign of innocence, since quite possibly nobody will speak up, yet you cannot simply ignore the matter (*B*). If the driver is accused of murder or rape, then do not hesitate to call in the police but in this case office supplies have been stolen. The police might well find no witnesses; even if they did, office harmony will have been destroyed. You are the boss and you will have to handle this. Start by knowing that such an accusation is unlikely to be fabricated: the staff member might be trying to ingratiate by informing you of the theft but he would have nothing to gain if it were untrue and he would risk the wrath of an angry driver. On the other hand, the staff member could be mistaken or perhaps unintentionally exaggerating a petty theft.

Before any of your staff can go sick or otherwise flee the scene, make it known to everybody in the office that they are to stay put until they are called, one by one, to see you. Then get the driver in. The last thing you want is for him to hear what is going on, before you are ready for him, and drive off with your Mercedes (or Toyota). Tell him that stock is missing and he has been accused. For once some straight speaking. If by chance he admits it, it would probably save a lot of trouble by letting him resign. If he denies it, have him wait outside your room. Let him hear you give orders for all stock records to be brought up. Make sure he sits there throughout your inquiry. Call all staff in one by one. Even if they have nothing to say keep them ten minutes. Having heard everybody and had the stock records or whatever other pieces of what might be evidence brought conspicuously into your room, decide if the driver is guilty or not before you call him in.

Even if you found no real evidence against him, don't immediately say so; if he is guilty, he probably thinks you have evidence—all those stock books open on your desk for a start. If he pleads not guilty but resigns on the spot, accept immediately. No notice, pay him off. If you have real evidence, tell him he has been seen by so many witnesses, etc. and that therefore you are dismissing him. No notice. Make sure he returns any keys, identification, etc. and get him out immediately. And know that your staff will credit you for your decision, you will probably have a happier office, since nobody likes tough guys. And know also that, even if the driver left humbly and gave you a *wai* (which you do not return!), you have made an enemy for life.

Score

A –10

B –5

C –4

D +5

E –5

SITUATION FIFTEEN

Your secretary, a reliable source of office gossip, tells you one day that the administration assistant is pushing for his brother to be recommended to you for employment in the vacant driver's job. He is treating the personnel officer, whom you rely on for recommendations, to lunch almost every day and at one lunch introduced his brother. Do you:

A Tick off the administration assistant and say that you cannot allow nepotism.

B Tell the personnel officer to remove the brother from the list of applicants.

C Wait until you get the recommendation, look at the other applicants and choose one.

D Tell your secretary to mind her own business.

E Pay special attention to selection and, with the personnel officer present, pick the one you consider the best candidate.

Comments

Duty to a brother comes before duty to the company: not that there need be any contradiction. It is perfectly normal (in a sense admirable) that the administration assistant wants to help his brother. So A is really out. B is almost as bad, since your action will be interpreted as criticism. Quietly choosing a different applicant, C, is neutral and nobody need lose face. If you are really against nepotism, that's for you. Your secretary, although she really knows what is acceptable and might or might not have questionable motives for her disclosure, at least came to tell you; probably she likes you, maybe she has been reading up on modern office management. Don't ever tell her to mind her own business. She probably does, but she minds your business as well. Go ahead and choose the best candidate, and if it's the administration assistant's brother … never mind and maybe so much the better.

Score

A −10

B −5

C 0

D −10

E +5

SITUATION SIXTEEN

You are visiting upcountry, examining the administration of a small, entirely Thai-manned new branch of your Bangkok based office. You know none of the staff personally. You have a budget of 7000 baht for the local purchase of a small refrigerator. Do you:

- A Tell the staff member responsible for administration that he should go out and buy a fridge up to 7000 baht and give you the receipt.
- B Send two members of staff independently to get quotations on fridges.
- C Send the administration officer to get specifications and prices so you can if necessary check with Bangkok and see if it is cheaper to send one up.
- D Buy it yourself.

Comments

You are the visiting boss. You do not go out and buy a fridge or anything else (*D*). Apart from the question of status, there is the pragmatic aspect of making such purchases after you are gone: this is your chance to see how your team will operate. Giving the administration officer full responsibility (*A*) is not a bad choice. You can always check later if the fridge really cost 7000 baht. However, this response does not make it clear to the administration officer that he, like you, is finally responsible to Bangkok office or Headquarters. Choice *C* sets out this structure without showing suspicion of anybody (as would be the case in *B*). It is as well to be careful. Trust your staff to a reasonable extent but be aware that if you quote a ceiling budget, receipts are likely to reflect that ceiling precisely to the baht.

Score

A 0
B –4
C +5
D –5

SITUATION SEVENTEEN

Visiting a reasonably important Thai for official or business matters in his office, you are received and invited to sit. A girl enters with a tray, sinks to her knees and places a cup of coffee and a glass of water in front of you. Your host has nothing. You do not drink coffee and are not thirsty. Do you:

    A Inform the girl that you would prefer tea.
    B Inform the host that you would prefer tea.
    C Leave both coffee and water untouched.
    D Drink the coffee rather than risk offence.
    E Take a sip of the coffee and leave the rest.
    F Drink the water and leave the coffee.

Comments

Puzzling over such petty etiquette shows at least that you are analysing situations. The offer of a glass of water is ubiquitous courtesy. There is no need to drink it. This courtesy has been extended to include coffee, which raises the status of the occasion. Whether you drink, sip or leave either or both will not offend or please your host. However, the coffee has been provided by the host so telling the girl to bring you tea (that is what it comes to) is not on. It is quite all right to tell the host you do not drink coffee, especially if you are to be a regular visitor, but say you prefer tea only if he asks. If either the girl or host asks you if you want coffee or tea, then you are of course free to state a preference or decline both.

It is traditional to wait until invited by the host before drinking. If you don't want to drink you can simply say 'thank you' and leave it at that.

Score

A –5

B –1

C 0

D 0

E 0

F 0

SITUATION EIGHTEEN

Returning from a successful field visit in the north of Thailand with some important local Thai business contacts, on your way for a social drink, everything around you stops moving as if spellstruck. The driver slows and looks at you for instructions. Faintly, through the glass windows, you hear loudspeakers. It is 6 p.m. Do you:

 A Ask the driver what is going on.
 B Tell the driver to pull over.
 C Say, 'Go on, what are you waiting for?'
 D Carry on speaking and leave the driving to the driver.
 E Tell the driver to stop immediately.

Comments

In rural areas more distant from Bangkok the national anthem is played over loudspeakers at 8 a.m. and 6 p.m. No need to pull over. Impress your associates and enjoy a quiet minute by stopping right in the middle of the road. Open the window and listen to the music. It is perhaps going too far to open your door and step out to attention. If you ignore this moment of simple national respect (*D*) you are showing at best your ignorance of local custom. You only have a minute, so asking the driver (*A*), while an understandable reaction, is an unnecessary waste of time—now that you know.

Score

A –1

B   0

C –5

D –2

E +5

TWENTY QUESTIONS

This true/false quiz is intended for children of all ages. Tick in either the true or false columns. One mark on your score for each correct answer, one mark off for each wrong answer. For those who find this too simple, supplementary questions are added in brackets. The quiz can be given verbally to several children at one time and they can be invited to add to the supplementary questions.

True   False

1. Eating in *Wat* grounds is forbidden. (Is any food forbidden to Thais?)

2. Shoes must be removed at the *Bot*. (Where else should shoes be removed?)

3. Menstruating women are not permitted inside the *Wat*. (What are the rules, if any, controlling entry?)

4. Monks do not eat after noon. (What are the 5 most important rules for monks?)

5. One should not sit cross-legged in audience with monks. (How does sitting position relate to status?)

6. Most Thais work in the rice fields. (What is Thailand's principal export?)

7. All Thais are called *Khun*. (How can *Khun* be translated in English?)

8. Only special friends should call a Thai by his nickname. (What is the likely origin of Thai nicknames?)

9. Hats should be removed when entering a Thai home. (Describe the relationship between hats and shoes.)

10. Most Thais use water and the left hand to clean their backsides after defecation. (How do toilet habits relate to social action?)

11 Thai Buddhist monks do not eat meat. (Why do they/don't they?)

12. It is forbidden for a woman to touch a monk or his robes. (How should a woman pass something to a monk?)

13. Hair is considered unclean by the Thais. (Explain the taboo against touching hair and heads.)

14. During Buddhist Lent, Thais do not drink alcohol. (When is Buddhist Lent?)

15. Anybody can become a monk. (What are the requirements?)

16. All Thai girls who wear cardigans back to front are defending themselves against evil spirits. (Why should such behaviour offer any protection?)

17. One Thai mother can compliment another on her 'ugly' baby. (How do childbirth ceremonies relate to belief in spirits?)

18. The inferior always pays for the superior. (What is the etiquette of paying in restaurants?)

239

19. Thais believe in fair criticism. (What are the 'ground rules' for indirect criticism?)
20. Thais generally feel that no problem is too big for them to tackle. (Describe Thai norms of conflict avoidance.)

Answers

True: Questions 2, 4, 5, 6, 9, 10, 12, 17
False: Questions 1, 3, 7, 8, 11, 13, 14, 15, 16, 18, 19, 20
No answers are given for supplementary questions, but they are all in this book somewhere.

Having read this book and completed the quiz, you will almost certainly find yourself in situations that we haven't covered. You are you and your situations are as unique as you are.

When you find yourself swimming in a new situation and you begin to get that sinking feeling, write your own quiz. Think of all your possible responses and, using your knowledge of Thai behaviour, evaluate these responses in positive and negative terms. Then follow the most positive alternative.

Some people find this approach to understanding a new culture somewhat over-analytical and even 'cold-blooded' or 'Machiavellian'. Others find it greatly increases their powers of awareness of what is going on around them and their place in it all. Perhaps the greatest benefit of this situationist approach to culture learning is that it can turn the most depressing situation into a game and even make it fun. Seen from this viewpoint, culture shock is both productive and positive, providing food for thought and action.

Life in Thailand is an endless, fascinating game. We have set out in this book some of the rules of this game. If there is one cardinal principle holding the whole glorious experience together, we would guess it is something like the sentence we cited in chapter 4 (page 78):

Life is very fun why quickly to go.

Have fun and you will survive forever.

HOW DO YOU DO AND TABOO

Affection between the sexes should not be displayed in public. No holding hands or kissing.

Avoid things, people and situations you don't like rather than moan about them or try to change them.

Beckon waiters and servants with the hand, palm downwards, fingers straight and waving rapidly. Don't clap, snap fingers or hiss.

Boasting is disliked, don't compare your country and people favourably with Thailand and the Thais.

Buddha images should be kept in a high place and treated with great respect. It is against the law to take or send them out of the country except under very special circumstances.

Ceremonies are normally open to everybody; at family ceremonies money is often given, inside an envelope, to the host or placed in the tray provided. Do not wear bright colours to a funeral.

Criticism: Avoid it; if absolutely unavoidable, balance with praise and be very indirect.

Discretion is admired as maturity; if you must do naughty things, do them in private.

Dress your status. Women do not wear shorts or revealing clothing.

Eating habits are flexible. Most people eat with a spoon and use a fork to load it. Salt is replaced by the liquid *nam pla* (fish sauce). During ceremonies always eat after the monks. Inviting to eat is an everyday greeting, the normal reply is 'eaten already'.

Feet must be kept to yourself. Not on the desk. Certainly not pointing at anybody. Do not step over anybody or anybody's food.

Flatter whenever possible, Thais love it.

Fun: The essential ingredient of anything worth doing; have it.

Generosity is the sign of an important person; don't be mean.

Gifts are to be opened in private.

Hair and heads should not be touched. If you do so by accident, excuse yourself.

Introductions are less frequent and more meaningful than in the west. Social inferior is addressed first.

Invitations are often less specific than in the west. If attendance and punctuality are important, use a card. If you specifically invite somebody to your house, they expect to eat there.

Laundry: If done by a man, don't be surprised if he refuses to wash a woman's underclothes.

Legs should not be crossed whether sitting on floor or chair in the presence of monks.

Lists of do and taboo such as this one are far from 100%. Think in terms of culture and situations rather than required and forbidden.

Lower the body a little when passing in front of, or between, people.

Monks are the most important people in the country and must be treated with respect at all times. Touching of a monk or his robes by a woman is strictly taboo.

Names: Use a person's first name, not the family name. Adults should be addressed as *Khun* unless a title is used.

Parties: Dress appropriately; do not wear black unless at funeral.

Pass objects with the right hand, touch left hand to right forearm if extra respect is required. Women never pass directly to monks.

Paying is done after eating/drinking, not before; the inviter pays; if no clear invitation, the superior pays; 'going Dutch' is very rare.

Please: See 'thank you'.

Pointing with fingers is acceptable for objects and animals but not for people.

Relax, take it easy, especially at the beginning of your stay.

Rice is the lifeblood of Thailand; don't throw it away in front of Thais.

Royalty must be treated with the greatest respect; stand up when images of the King or Royal Family appear on the cinema screen.

Shoes come off at the door of the main temple building and at all homes.

Sit in the place you are directed to. Superiors in front, inferiors at the back.

Speak gently, do not raise the voice.

Smile and people will like you. A smile can be used to excuse small inconveniences, to thank for small services and to return the *wai* of children and servants.

Tempers must be kept.

Thank you, like 'please', is expressed verbally much less frequently in Thai; a smile is often enough.

Throwing any object is bad manners.

Titles are always used.

Visiting homes without specific invitation is normal; gifts of fruit, cakes, flowers, etc. are appreciated but not necessary. Shoes off unless requested to keep them on. Casual visitors should be invited to drink and, if mealtime, to eat.

Wai monks, old people and your social superiors. Do not *wai* servants, labourers and children. The lower the head, the more respect is shown. The inferior initiates the *wai*. Whatever the *wai* received, reply with a lesser one.

Walk slightly behind monks and old people.

BIBLIOGRAPHY

Branchard, W., *Thailand: Its People, Its Society, Its Culture*, New Haven, HRAF Press, 1958. Now somewhat dated but still one of the most comprehensive books on Thailand.

Cooper, R., *Thais Mean Business*, Singapore, Times Books International. A humorous A—Z for the expat manager and businessman in Thailand.

Hollinger, C., *Mai Pen Rai Means Never Mind*, Bangkok, Asia Books. An autobiographical account of an expat's experiences living and teaching in Thailand. The funniest and best introduction to the Thais available. It will help you enjoy your culture shock.

Insight Photo Guides, *Thailand*. Updated every year, certainly the most useful and beautiful of the many guide books to Thailand.

Klausner, W., *Conflict and Communication*, Bangkok. Deals specifically with the meeting between Thai and *farang*. Very readable and informative. A must for expat businessmen.

Kukrit Pramoj, *Red Bamboo*, Bangkok, Progress Publishing Co. The ex-Prime Minister of Thailand authors this very readable novel about Thai villagers. The story is identical to the Don Camillo series, but the characters come through as 100 per cent Thai.

Mulder, N., *Everyday Life in Thailand: An Interpretation*, Bangkok, Editions Duang Kamol. One for the specialist. Mulder writes for the Thai scholar. If you already have quite a good knowledge of Thai society, this book could increase it.

Phya Anuman Rajadhon. A huge collection of books and pamphlets on many aspects of Thai culture. Concentrates on ceremony. Just ask for his works at any good bookshop or library.

Segaller, D., *Thai Ways*, and *More Thai Ways* Bangkok Post Publishing. A must. These books reprint articles on Thai culture published in the *Bangkok World* since 1975. They are a mine of information, open them anywhere and you learn something new.

THE AUTHORS

Robert and Nanthapa claim Chiengmai as their spiritual home. It was there that they met in April 1978, when Nanthapa was working with an agriculture development agency and Robert was updating doctoral research he had completed three years earlier when he lived for two years with the Hmong and other hill tribes of northern Thailand, studying their economic anthropology. Both have travelled, studied and worked widely in *farang* and Asian worlds.

In 1980 Robert left an academic career in anthropology that included lectureships and fellowships at Singapore, Chulalongkorn and Chiang Mai universities to join the United Nations High Commissioner for Refugees. He has served with the UN in Laos, Geneva, Malawi, the Philippines, Bangkok, Chiang Kham in Northern Thailand, Nepal Bangladesh and Indonesia.

In addition to writings on Thai culture, he has written two books on the Hmong: *Resource Scarcity and the Hmong Response* and *The Hmong* (Times Editions). He is the author of the companion volume to *Culture Shock! Thailand, Thais Mean Business* (Times Editions), in which he encourages the expat manager working in Thailand towards a middle path of hands-off management.

INDEX